NEGLIGENCE IN VALUATIONS
AND SURVEYS

NEGLIGENCE IN VALUATIONS AND SURVEYS

John Murdoch

Published by RICS Business Services Limited
a wholly owned subsidiary of
The Royal Institution of Chartered Surveyors
under the RICS Books imprint
Surveyor Court
Westwood Business Park
Coventry CV4 8JE
UK

ISBN 1 84219 072 5

Reprinted 2005

Typeset in Great Britain by Columns Design Ltd, Reading
Printed in Great Britain by Bell & Bain Ltd, Glasgow

Contents

Preface

I have always maintained that, while chartered surveyors do not need the *breadth* of understanding of the law of their opposite numbers in the legal profession, in a number of key areas of application to property and construction they need a similar *depth* of legal knowledge. As an External Examiner at the University of Reading, I have noticed with interest that certain modular subjects are taken by both Land Management and Law Students. I regard this as entirely proper. Exactly what the key areas may be depends to some extent on the nature of the surveyor's practice (although it is not an accident that the subject of this first handbook of the Case in Point series is one which concerns members of all the Royal Institution of Chartered Surveyors (RICS) Faculties, and indeed of all disciplines). Two obvious examples are the law of landlord and tenant and town and country planning, and I have met plenty of surveyors who know much more about rent reviews or compulsory purchase compensation than the average lawyer in general practice.

So surveyors need law, and for a variety of reasons need to develop their understanding of it. Changing trends or individual variations in clients' requirements mean that from time to time even the best practitioners (perhaps especially the best practitioners) will feel the need to expand their knowledge. The knowledge acquired at college or in studying for the Assessment of Professional Competence has a limited shelf life and needs to be constantly updated to maintain its currency. Even specialists working in their areas of expertise need a source of reference as an aide-memoire or as a first port of call in more detailed research.

The Case in Point Series

RICS Books is committed to meeting the needs of surveying (and other) professionals and the Case in Point series typifies that commitment. It is aimed at those who need to upgrade their legal knowledge, or update it, or have access to a good first reference at the outset of an inquiry. A particular difficulty is the burgeoning of reported decisions of the courts. The sheer scale of the law reports, both general and specialist, makes it very hard even to be aware of recent trends, let alone identify the significance of a particular decision. Thus it was decided to focus on developments in case law. In any given matter, the practitioner will want to be directed efficiently and painlessly to the decision which bears upon the matter which he or she is dealing with, in other words to – the Case in Point.

The series offers a wealth of legal information which is essential in its practical application to the surveyor's work. The author of each title has the high level of expertise required to be selective and succinct; thus achieving a high degree of relevancy without sacrificing accessibility. The series will develop incrementally until it comprises a collection of specialist handbooks which can deliver what busy practitioners need – the law on the matter they are handling, when they want it.

Negligence in Valuations and Surveys, John Murdoch

The series has started with one of the most respected legal authors known to the surveying profession. This subject was chosen for the first publication in the Case in Point series advisedly. Whereas some of the most eligible topics for inclusion in the series, such as those in landlord and tenant, are of interest only to a proportion of practitioners, albeit a significant one, professional liability is of concern to all.

It is axiomatic that the concern derives from the fact that almost everyone, at one time or another, has done something which a court of law would regard as negligent. A case like *Merrett v Babb*, decided by the Court of Appeal in 2001, certainly adds piquancy to that concern, because it decides that the consequences of a finding of negligence can be brought home personally to a valuer deprived of the protection of professional indemnity insurance by his firm's insolvency.

What John Murdoch's treatment of the subject does is to demystify it and provide a tool-kit for dealing with it. This Case in Point handbook will enable the practitioner to review his or her position either before entering into a commitment or when some allegation has been made, and to take a view of the exposure involved, if any. The sections of the work correspond to the principal questions which have to be answered in that process and provide answers to them. Not always final definitive answers, because that will sometimes require further research, including resort to the full, original case reports and where there may be liability legal advice will need to be taken and insurers notified. But in most situations, the practitioner will be able to obtain at least a preliminary view of the position to be addressed and often a good idea of the likely outcome, from this one source. This is a considerable achievement.

Anthony Lavers,
Professional Support Lawyer, White & Case, London, 2002.
Consultant Editor, Case in Point Series.

Introduction

Once upon a time, the members of learned professions enjoyed an aura, if not of inevitability, then at least of unchallengeability. No longer: in our increasingly consumerist and compensation-conscious age, professionals from surgeons to accountants are viewed as mere service-providers, with the same obligation as to the standard of those services as a greengrocer bears for the quality of his vegetables. No profession is exempt (even the long-standing immunity of barristers and other advocates has recently been swept away), and surveyors and valuers are finding themselves in the firing line in every aspect of their work.

Fifty years ago, the vast majority of reported actions brought against the property professions arose out of residential building surveys. Today, the picture is very different: residential mortgage valuations, once regarded by general practitioners as a safe, albeit modest, source of income, have become a very thorny thicket, as both lender clients and house purchasers have been quick to pounce on any error in the report and to turn on the surveyor. Even more worrying, in terms of the size of claims and their potential impact on professional indemnity insurance premiums, has been the growth in claims by financial institutions which, having lent on the security of commercial property when times were good, learn to their cost that markets fall as well as rise, and seek to lay off their losses on their professional advisers (especially valuers) when their property company borrowers default.

Not surprisingly, in view of their increasing exposure, valuers and surveyors want to understand the framework of legal liabilities which surrounds their work. This book aims to provide such an understanding, in a form which busy professionals can easily assimilate. The emphasis throughout is on actual cases in which valuers and surveyors have been sued, and which have laid down the principles of liability by which they must live (or die). A practitioner seeking guidance on a particular issue will find a brief passage of text and a group of relevant cases, followed by an explanation of the salient point of each case. This should be sufficient to identify those cases which are of special relevance and hence worth reading in full, a task simplified by the Table of Cases.

Following this brief introduction, the remainder of the book is divided into five main sections. The first, entitled 'Duty of Care', seeks to answer the question: 'Who is entitled to hold a valuer or surveyor liable for negligence?' The most obvious answer to this question is: 'the client', but it is not the only possible answer. For almost 40 years, the law has recognized the possibility that a professional adviser may also be held liable to certain other parties who are not clients, provided that there is a sufficiently close relationship between them.

The second section, entitled 'Breach of Duty', is concerned with identifying the kind of acts or omissions which will be held to constitute negligence; or, to put it another way, the standards of care and skill that a surveyor or valuer is expected to achieve. This section describes the legal principles applicable to professional negligence in general, before dealing with those reported cases which are of specific relevance to valuers or surveyors.

The third section, entitled 'Extent of Liability', deals with the way in which damages are quantified in cases involving negligent surveys or valuations. Again, this begins by outlining the general principles of assessment, before turning to the specific rules which apply to claims by vendors and purchasers, mortgage lenders and others.

In legal terms, a claimant who can satisfy the court that there was a duty of care, breach of that duty and resulting damage or loss has done all that is required to succeed in an action for negligence. However, the focus then switches to the defendant, who may be able in various ways to avoid being held liable. The fourth section of the book, entitled 'Defences', deals with two particular ways in which liability may thus be avoided. The first of these is by means of an exemption clause or disclaimer, which, if it is to be effective, must satisfy various stringent rules laid down by both common law and statute (notably the Unfair Contract Terms Act 1977). The second concerns the time limits within which various types of legal action must be commenced; if a relevant time limit is not met, then the claim is statute-barred and will fail.

The fifth and final section of the book, entitled 'Shifting the Blame', concerns three other defences or quasi-defences, whose common thread is that they all involve the defendant in passing some or all of the legal responsibility on to someone else (either the claimant or a third party). The most significant (and most frequently used) of these is the defence of contributory negligence, under which the valuer or surveyor argues that the claimant is partly to blame for his or her own losses. Less common (though more drastic when it does apply) is the principle of mitigation, under which it is argued that a particular aspect of the claimant's loss is entirely his or her own fault. Finally, there is the possibility that the defendant, while not avoiding responsibility altogether, may be able to shift part of the liability on to a third party, such as one of the claimant's other professional advisers.

Table of Cases

Table of Cases

1
Duty of Care

A valuer or surveyor who carries out professional work will owe a duty of care and skill to the client, as an express or implied term of the contract under which the work is to be done. If the work is not carried out to the required standards of reasonable care and skill, the client may also be entitled to claim under the tort of negligence. This can be an important option in relation to the time limits within which a legal claim must be started. Moreover, an action in tort for negligence may also be available to certain persons who are not clients, provided that their relationship with the valuer or surveyor is a sufficiently 'proximate' one.

1.1 DUTY TO THE CLIENT

1.1.1 Duty in contract

The law does not require a contract between surveyor or valuer and client to be made in any particular form. Hence, it makes no difference whether instructions are given in writing or by word of mouth (although written instructions will of course be easier to prove in the event of a dispute). Moreover, the rules of a professional institution may require its members to ensure that their instructions are given or confirmed in writing.

RICS *Appraisal and Valuation Manual,* Practice Statement 2

A member of the Royal Institution of Chartered Surveyors (RICS) must seek to establish the client's requirements, including the purpose of the valuation, so as to ensure that an appropriate basis of valuation is used. The valuer must always agree or confirm in writing certain aspects of the service to be provided, including the property to be valued, the date and basis of the valuation and any assumptions to be made.

The contract will normally define the task to be performed and may also describe the standards to be achieved. If it does not, these standards will be set by terms implied by law.

Supply of Goods and Services Act 1982, s. 13

In a contract for the supply of a service where the supplier is acting in the course of a business (which includes a profession), there is an implied term that the supplier will carry out the service with reasonable care and skill.

Supply of Goods and Services Act 1982, s. 14

Where, under a contract for the supply of a service by a supplier acting in the course of a business (which includes a profession), the time for the service to be carried out is not fixed by the contract, left to be fixed in a manner agreed by the contract or determined by the course of dealing between the parties, there is an implied term that the supplier will carry out the service within a reasonable time.

Where a client instructs a firm of surveyors or valuers, the contract will normally be made with the firm, rather than with an individual member of that firm. (As to whether the individual employee who actually carries out the work might also be liable in tort, see *Merrett* v *Babb*, section 1.2.2 a, below). The firm will be responsible for an individual, whether or not employed by them, to whom the work is entrusted.

Luxmoore-May v Messenger May Baverstock (1990)

It was held by the Court of Appeal that a firm of provincial auctioneers which took on the task of attributing and valuing a painting would be liable for any negligence by a self-employed 'consultant' to whom the firm delegated that task.

A surveyor or valuer will be entitled, as an express or implied term of the contract with the client, to a fee for professional services. However, if negligence means that those services are worthless, no fee is payable.

Whitty v Lord Dillon (1860)

A valuer who valued the timber on an estate on an entirely erroneous basis, with the result that his valuation was inaccurate by almost 50%, was held not to be entitled to his agreed fee.

Chong v Scott Collins & Co. (1954)

The client of a building surveyor was held entitled to recover the fees which he had paid, on the ground that the survey had been so negligently carried out as to be of no practical use.

1.1.2 Duty in tort

In certain respects, most notably the time by which legal proceedings must be started if they are not to be statute-barred (see section 4.2 below), there may be significant advantages to be gained from bringing a legal action in the tort of negligence rather than for breach of contract.

South Australia Asset Management Corp. v York Montague Ltd (1996)

It was said by the House of Lords that, where a valuer owes a contractual duty of care and skill to a client, he or she will also owe that client a concurrent duty in tort. Unless there are exceptional circumstances, the *scope* of these two duties will be the same.

1.2 DUTY TO THIRD PARTIES

1.2.1 General principles

According to a long-standing legal principle known as 'privity of contract', rights or obligations created by a contract can only be enforced by or against the parties to that contract. Until recently, English law had always adhered rigidly to this principle, but statute now recognizes the possibility that, in certain limited circumstances, contractual rights may be conferred upon third parties.

Contracts (Rights of Third Parties) Act 1999, s. 1

A person who is not party to a contract may nevertheless enforce a term of that contract if *either* the contract expressly provides that he may do so *or* the term in question 'purports to confer a benefit on him' and there is nothing in the contract to suggest that the parties did not intend the third party to be able to enforce it. For this to apply, the third party must be expressly identified in the contract by name, as a member of a class or as answering a particular description.

A principle of enormous practical significance in the context of professional negligence is that which was laid down by the House of Lords in *Hedley Byrne & Co. Ltd* v *Heller & Partners Ltd* (1964). It was there held that a person who provides advice may owe a duty of care to someone with whom he or she does not have a contract, provided that the parties are in a 'special relationship'. What exactly this means is not entirely clear; one school of thought would require evidence of a 'voluntary assumption of responsibility' by the adviser, another would merely require there to be a relationship of 'proximity' in circumstances where it would be 'just and reasonable' to impose a duty of care.

In accordance with this principle, a surveyor or valuer may owe a duty of care to someone who he or she knows or ought to know is likely to rely on their report, but not to someone of whose reliance he or she has no knowledge and no reason to know.

Smith v Carter (1994)

Wherever a mortgage valuer would owe a duty of care to a house purchaser (see section 1.2.2 below), he or she will owe the same duty to two joint purchasers, even though the valuer may have been completely unaware that the property was to be jointly purchased. This is because such arrangements are common in the housing market, and the valuer can therefore reasonably be expected to foresee them.

Le Lievre v Gould (1893)

A surveyor was instructed and paid by a builder to issue certificates confirming the latter's progress on a particular building project. The builder passed these certificates to a lender, who then advanced appropriate parts of the agreed price for the works. It was held by the Court of Appeal that the surveyor owed no duty of care to the lender, since he did not know and had no reason to know that the certificates were to be used for this purpose.

1.2.2 Duty of lender's valuer to borrower

(a) *Position of valuer*

A valuer who inspects property on behalf of a mortgage lender may owe a duty of care, not only to the lender, but also to the purchaser. This applies not only where the inspection is carried out by an independent valuer, but also where it is done in-house, that is, where the valuer is an employee of the lender. It makes no difference whether or not the content of the valuer's report is actually disclosed to the purchaser; even if it is not, the purchaser can assume, from the mere fact that the mortgage loan is approved, that the property must have been valued at no less than the amount of the loan. It is possible, however, that the principle does not extend to cases of very substantial (especially commercial) property. This is because a purchaser of such property may be reasonably expected to instruct, pay and rely upon his or her own advisers, rather than upon someone who is instructed and paid by the lender.

Yianni v Edwin Evans & Sons (1982)

A firm of valuers was instructed by a building society to inspect and report on a modest Victorian house, which was purchased in 1975 for £15,000. The valuers were held liable to the purchaser (who did not see the report) for negligently failing to discover a serious subsidence problem. The court reached this decision despite the presence of clear warnings in the building society's standard loan documentation to the effect that purchasers should not rely on the mortgage valuation but should commission their own survey. This was because the evidence showed that 90% of house purchasers (at least at the lower end of the housing market) routinely ignored such warnings.

Smith v Eric S Bush (1990)

A firm of valuers was instructed by a building society to inspect and report on a modest house which was purchased in 1980 for £18,000. The valuers were held liable to the purchaser for negligently failing to discover that the chimneys had been left unsupported following the removal of the chimney breasts. In this case the purchaser, who required a mortgage of approximately 20% of the purchase price, was shown a copy of the valuer's report. The House of Lords regarded the imposition of a duty of care to the purchaser as fair and reasonable, given that the valuer's fee for the inspection came, at least indirectly, out of the purchaser's pocket.

Harris v Wyre Forest DC (1990)

In this case, which was heard together with *Smith* v *Bush*, the House of Lords held a local authority lender vicariously liable to the purchasers of a modest house (purchased in 1978 for £9,000) for the negligence of a member of its staff. This employee, on inspecting the property, failed to discover that it was subject to serious subsidence and required extensive underpinning. In this case the purchasers did not see the inspector's report but they were able to work out, from the amount of the loan which they were offered, the minimum at which it must have been valued.

Where a mortgage valuation is carried out by an employee of a firm, any legal action for negligence will normally be brought against the firm by which he or she is employed. However, it seems that the individual valuer is potentially also liable.

Merrett v Babb (2001)

The defendant, a qualified surveyor who was employed by a firm of valuers, carried out a mortgage valuation for a building society and signed the valuation report in his own name. By the time that the house purchaser sought to bring an action for negligence on the basis of this report, the firm had become insolvent, with the consequence that its professional indemnity insurance policy had been cancelled. The Court of Appeal held by a majority that the purchaser was entitled to recover damages from the defendant personally, despite the fact that the purchaser had not actually seen the valuer's report and was unaware, at the time of purchase, of his identity.

(b) *Position of lender*

As a general principle, a mortgage lender is not legally responsible to a house purchaser for the negligence of an independent valuer who is instructed by the lender to inspect and value the property for mortgage purposes. However, in certain circumstances the lender may indirectly incur liability for such negligence.

Harris v Wyre Forest DC (1990)

The House of Lords held that, where a mortgage valuation is carried out by an employee of the lending institution, the lender may be vicariously liable just like any other employer if it is carried out negligently.

Ward v McMaster (1985)

Where a mortgage lender commissions a valuation from an independent valuer, it owes a duty of care to the purchaser to select one who is competent to perform the task. If the lender negligently selects an incompetent valuer, it may be liable to the purchaser for the resulting loss.

Beresforde v Chesterfield BC (1989)

Where a mortgage lender 'adopts' the report of an independent valuer (for example, by copying it on its own notepaper before sending it to the house purchaser) this may possibly be enough to make the lender responsible to the purchaser if the valuer has been negligent.

1.2.3 Duty of borrower's valuer to lender

In the case of loans secured on commercial property, it is not uncommon for the lender to rely on a valuation of the property which has been commissioned and paid for by the prospective borrower. Where the valuer knows the identity of the lender to whom the valuation will be passed on (for example, where the report is specifically readdressed to the lender), it seems clear that a duty of care will be owed. However, the position is less clear cut where the valuer is aware of the lender's existence but not of his or her identity (for example, where the known recipient of the valuation is not the ultimate lender). Here the courts have reached some conflicting decisions. The position may be further complicated where the valuation itself contains a provision which purports to restrict its use to the addressee (see section 4.1.1 below).

Cann v Willson (1888)

A valuer, having carried out a valuation of property for a prospective borrower, sent his report to the lender's solicitor in the knowledge that the lender would rely on it. It was held that the valuer owed the lender a duty of care.

Banque Bruxelles Lambert SA v Eagle Star Insurance Co. Ltd (1994)

Valuers who valued property for a borrower were held to owe a duty of care to both the lender and the insurance company which issued a mortgage indemnity guarantee policy, since the valuers knew that both these parties would rely on their valuation.

Nightingale Finance Ltd v White & Co. (1997)

Valuers sent a mortgage valuation to the company which they believed was to be the lender, but the actual mortgage loan was made by a subsidiary of that company. It was held that the valuers owed a duty of care to the subsidiary.

Assured Advances Ltd v Ashbee & Co. (1994)

Where valuers were instructed by mortgage brokers, knowing that a decision on lending would be based on their valuation, it was said that they would owe a duty of care to the ultimate lender, even if the valuation was passed from hand to hand until a lender could be found.

Secured Residential Funding plc v Nationwide Building Society (1997)

A mortgage valuation was commissioned by a company which the valuers believed to be the intended lender, when in reality that company was acting as an agent for the true lender. It was held that, as far as the tort of negligence was concerned, the valuers owed no duty of care to the lender, of whose existence they were completely unaware.

Secured Residential Funding plc v Nationwide Building Society (No 2) (1998)

In a completely separate case on similar facts, which happened to concern the same parties, it was held that the unknown lender was an 'undisclosed principal'. Accordingly, the lender could sue the valuers under the law of agency for breach of the contract which had been made by the agent on its behalf.

1.2.4 Duty of vendor's surveyor to purchaser

In certain circumstances (for example, where property is to be sold by auction), a vendor may commission a survey report with the intention of making this available to prospective purchasers. Provided that the surveyor knows what is intended, it seems that he or she may owe a duty of care to a purchaser who relied on the report.

Shankie-Williams v Heavey (1986)

A vendor, having completed the conversion of a house into three flats, commissioned an inspection of the floorboards and underfloor timbers of the ground-floor flat from a dry rot surveying specialist, making it clear that he wanted a report that he could show to prospective purchasers. It was held that the surveyor, who negligently reported that there was no evidence of dry rot, owed a duty of care to the purchasers of the ground-floor flat. However, no duty was owed to the purchaser of the flat above, who was shown the surveyor's report and concluded from it that this flat must also be free from dry rot.

1.2.5 Duty of mortgagee's surveyor to mortgagor

When a borrower defaults in mortgage repayments, the lender is usually entitled to repossess and resell the mortgaged property. In so doing, the lender owes a duty to the borrower not to sell at less than the market value. Breach of this duty entitles the borrower to recover damages from the lender. Some judges have suggested that, where the sale at an undervalue is the fault of the lender's professional advisers, the borrower might also be entitled to sue that adviser. However, not every judge agrees.

Cuckmere Brick Co. Ltd v Mutual Finance Ltd (1971)

Repossessed property was sold at an undervalue, due to the negligence of the auctioneers who were handling the sale for the lenders. The Court of Appeal held the lenders liable to the borrowers, and one of the judges stated that the auction-eers would, if sued, also have been liable.

Huish v Ellis (1995)

It was held that a surveyor advising a mortgage lender on resale owed no duty of care to the borrower to see that the property realized its market value. The judge thought that the imposition of such a duty would create an undesirable conflict of interest for the surveyor, and that it would be in any case unnecessary, since the borrower would be sufficiently protected by his or her rights against the lender.

1.2.6 Duty of arbitrators and independent experts

A contract relating to real property may provide that, if a certain type of dispute arises between the parties, they will submit this to an independent third party (who may be nominated by the parties themselves or by someone else, such as the President of the RICS) for determination. Such provisions are common, for example, in the context of rent reviews. The decision-maker may be either an arbitrator or an 'independent expert'; the category into which he or she falls will determine whether or not he or she owes a duty of care to the parties and will also affect the enforceability of the decision itself.

(a) *Duty of care*

Arbitration Act 1996, s. 29 (1)

Arbitrators are not liable for anything done or omitted in the carrying out of their functions, unless they are shown to have acted in bad faith.

Zubaida v Hargreaves (1995)

Independent experts owe a duty to both parties to make their valuation and consequent decision with reasonable care and skill. If they fail to do so, they will be liable to whichever party has to pay more or receive less than they should have done.

Curry Group plc v Martin (1999)

It was held that there is no difference in standard between the duty of care which is owed by a valuer to his or her client and the duty of care which is owed by an independent expert to both parties.

(b) *Enforceability*

Arbitration Act 1996, s. 69 (1)

Unless the parties agree otherwise, a party who is dissatisfied with the decision of an arbitrator may appeal to the court on a point of law.

Jones v Sherwood Computer Services plc (1992)

Where a contract gives an independent expert exclusive jurisdiction to determine a particular question, and provides that the parties are to be bound by the determination, the expert's decision cannot be set aside merely because his or her reasoned determination can be shown to contain errors of law. The decision can, however, be challenged where the expert has gone outside his or her jurisdiction, for example, by answering the wrong question.

National Grid Co. plc v M25 Group Ltd (1998)

The Court of Appeal held that, on the correct interpretation of the rent review provisions in a particular lease, an independent expert had exclusive jurisdiction over the 'valuation question', but did not have the exclusive power to interpret the lease terms defining the basis on which the rent review was to be made. As a result, the court could give a ruling on such matters, at least before a 'non-speaking' valuation had been made.

Morgan Sindall plc v Sawston Farms (Cambs) Ltd (1999)

Irrespective of the principles outlined above, a 'non-speaking' valuation by an independent expert is virtually impossible to challenge once it has been made. It was said that a court should give no encouragement to any attempt to infer, from the decision given, what the basis of that decision must have been and then to argue that the basis was incorrect.

2
Breach of Duty

2.1 GENERAL PRINCIPLES

2.1.1 Defining the task

In any professional negligence case, the liability of a valuer or surveyor will depend upon whether he or she has acted with reasonable care and skill. However, while this is in principle a universal standard, its detailed application will naturally vary with the facts of each individual case. In particular, much will depend upon the service that the defendant has undertaken to provide. For example, common sense suggests that a surveyor who is carrying out a full building survey must spend more time and give more attention to detail than if he or she were carrying out a mortgage valuation. It follows that the agreement between client and professional must be carefully interpreted, in order to identify precisely what service was to be carried out. In a number of cases, a professional has been able to avoid liability on the ground that he or she had undertaken to provide only a limited service.

Arab Bank plc v John D Wood (Commercial) Ltd (2000)

The court decided that what a firm of valuers had agreed to carry out was not a full free-standing open market valuation of a large and complex industrial estate. It was rather a 'franking valuation', that is a check on a valuation which had been provided earlier by another firm. It was held accordingly that the second valuers were entitled to accept the factual content of the earlier report (such matters as floor areas and physical condition), except in so far as the very limited inspection of the property which they themselves had carried out might cause them to doubt the accuracy of the information.

Beaumont v Humberts (1990)

The defendants were instructed to value 'for insurance rein-statement purposes' a Grade II listed house, parts of which were 300 years old. The Court of Appeal was divided over the question of whether the word 'reinstatement' in this con-text meant exact replication of the existing structure, the provision of a modern house offering equivalent accommo-dation, or something in-between these two meanings.

Predeth v Castle Phillips Finance Co. Ltd (1986)

A mortgage lender asked a valuer for a 'crash sale valuation' of a property which it had recently repossessed when the borrower defaulted. The lender resold the property at slightly more than the figure provided by the valuer, but was subsequently held liable to the borrower for failing to obtain the best available price. The lender then sued the valuer for negligence in failing to advise it as to the true market value of the property! This claim was rejected by the Court of Appeal, on the ground that the valuer had provided exactly what the lender had asked for, namely an indication of what the property might fetch if sold under extreme forced sale conditions.

Sutcliffe v Sayer (1987)

The prospective purchasers of a bungalow asked a local estate agent to advise them as to whether the asking price was about right, in view of local market conditions. The agent confirmed that the price was appropriate, but failed to point out that the ground on which the property was built might well render it difficult to resell. It was held that this omission did not make the agent guilty of negligence, since he had satisfactorily provided the limited service which had been requested.

McIntyre v Herring Son & Daw (1988)

A private client asked the defendants' specialist rating department to assist him in seeking a reduction in the rate-able value of his leasehold house. The defendants were successful in achieving a substantial reduction, but did not point out to the client that, if a small further reduction could be achieved (something which would require him to take legal proceedings) the property would then fall within the Leasehold Reform Act 1967 and the client would be entitled to purchase the freehold at a discounted price. It was held that the defendants were negligent in not giving the client this information, even though their instructions had nothing to do with leasehold enfranchisement. This decision, which is in stark contrast to the two cases noted above, appears to have been heavily influenced by the fact that the defendants were specialists in the field and the client was a private individual.

2.1.2 The basic standard

In an action for professional negligence, the standard by which the defendant falls to be judged is that of the ordinary competent member of the relevant profession.

Watts v Savills (1998)

The specific allegation of negligence made against a valuer who advised a vendor of agricultural land was that he had failed to appreciate the potential of that land for residential development. In rejecting (by a majority) this allegation, the Court of Appeal pointed out that the defendant could only be held liable 'if no reasonably competent valuer, acting carefully, could have formed the view that it had no development potential'.

Kenney v Hall, Pain & Foster (1976)

The fact that a valuation was carried out for no fee was held to be no justification for reducing the standard of care and skill which the valuer was expected to achieve.

Private Bank & Trust Co. Ltd v S (UK) Ltd (1993)

It was pointed out that the standard demanded of a valuer is not to be reduced on the ground that the valuation is carried out in difficult circumstances, for example, where the market is showing signs of collapsing into a depression.

The basic standard of care and skill is an objective one, in the sense that it does not vary according to the experience and/or qualifications of the individual concerned.

Freeman v Marshall & Co. (1966)

The defendant, in carrying out a survey, failed to report on rising damp. When sued for negligence, the defendant claimed to be unqualified, to have had no professional training and to have only a working knowledge of structures from an estate agency point of view. It was held that, since the defendant described himself as a surveyor when taking on work, he must be judged by the standards of a qualified surveyor.

Kenney v Hall, Pain & Foster (1976)

The defendant estate agents were held responsible for a free valuation of the claimant's house, given to the claimant by an inexperienced and unqualified negotiator who chose not to seek assistance from a more senior colleague. The fact that the individual was inexperienced and unqualified did not justify the application of a more relaxed standard of care and skill.

Baxter v FW Gapp & Co. Ltd (1938)

A valuer who carried out a mortgage valuation in an area of which he had no particular knowledge was held to have been negligent in failing to take account of certain comparable properties. The defendant was unaware of these, but they would almost certainly have been familiar to a local practitioner. (It should be noted that lack of relevant local knowledge would now constitute a breach of the RICS *Appraisal and Valuation Manual*, Practice Statement 5.)

2.1.3 Guidance from professional institutions

When dealing with an allegation of negligence against a surveyor or valuer, a court will pay close attention to any relevant RICS Practice Statements, Guidance Notes and similar documents. These will be treated as highly persuasive (though not conclusive) evidence of the kind of standards that a competent member of the profession can reasonably be expected to achieve.

PK Finans International (UK) Ltd v Andrew Downs & Co. Ltd (1992)

The court stated that:

> These Guidance Notes are not to be regarded as a statute. I suspect they are as much for the protection of surveyors as anything else, in that they set out various recommendations ... In any event, mere failure to comply with the Guidance Notes does not necessarily constitute negligence.

Watts v Morrow (1991)

The court was highly critical of a building surveyor who (contrary to the relevant RICS guidance) dictated his report during his inspection, rather than making notes on site which could subsequently be given further reflective consideration while being used as the basis of his actual report.

Hacker v Thomas Deal & Co. (1991)

A building surveyor who did not use a mirror to check for damp behind kitchen cupboards was held not negligent, since the relevant RICS guidance specifically treated the use of a mirror as a matter of individual choice.

Craneheath Securities Ltd v York Montague Ltd (1994)

The court relied on the relevant RICS guidance in holding that a mortgage valuer had been entitled to use 'open market value' as the basis for his valuation of a restaurant.

Allied Trust Bank Ltd v Edward Symmons & Partners (1994)

The court relied on the relevant RICS guidance in holding that a mortgage valuer had been entitled to include an element of 'hope value' in his valuation of a country house which had clear development potential.

RICS *Appraisal and Valuation Manual*

This contains 23 Practice Statements (seven general, the rest dealing with particular types of valuation) with which members of the RICS are bound to comply. They are primarily concerned, not with valuation theory or methods, but with the framework of good practice: establishing and understanding the client's requirements; being equipped to meet those requirements; assembling and interpreting relevant information and providing appropriate advice in an unambiguous and comprehensible form. The Manual also contains a series of Guidance Notes, which provide further advice on good valuation practice, but which are not formally binding on members of the RICS.

2.1.4 Legal knowledge

Valuers and surveyors are not expected to have the same degree of expertise in the law as solicitors or barristers. However, they are expected to have an understanding of the legal principles which underpin different types of valuation or other professional work (such as definition of 'disrepair' in a schedule of dilapidations).

Jenkins v Betham (1855)

The test for dilapidations in ecclesiastical property was the cost of putting the premises into good and substantial repair, rather than the cost of rendering the premises habitable (the test applicable to normal leases). The defendant, in carrying out a valuation of dilapidations in a rectory, was held guilty of negligence in failing to apply the correct legal standard, since this should be well known to any surveyor holding himself out as competent to carry out such work.

Corisand Investments Ltd v Druce & Co. (1978)

The defendants, in valuing a hotel, were held negligent for failing to take into account the cost of works which would be needed to satisfy the Fire Precautions Act 1971, and thus to obtain a fire certificate.

Theodore Goddard v Fletcher King Services Ltd (1997)

Solicitors, in drafting a lease on behalf of the landlords of commercial property, were instructed to ensure that it provided for upwards only rent reviews; however, they failed to do so. The landlords' managing surveyors, to whom the lease was sent for approval, failed to notice the error. It was held (rather harshly, perhaps) that the surveyors were guilty of negligence, although the solicitors had to bear the greater share of responsibility to their clients for this error.

2.1.5 Currency of expertise

A defendant accused of negligence in the course of a survey or valuation must be judged according to professional standards and knowledge at the time that the work in question was carried out. This is two-edged: the defendant must not be judged over-harshly, on the basis of hindsight but, on the other hand, many professionals have been found liable for failing to keep their knowledge and expertise up to date.

Private Bank & Trust Co. Ltd v S (UK) Ltd (1993)

It was specifically noted that the court must be careful to guard against hindsight and to determine the surveyor's skill and competence on the knowledge and information available to him at the time of the survey. Thus, where a valuation of an office development was carried out shortly before a sudden and severe fall in the commercial property market, it was held that the valuer had not been negligent:

> Though the market was going through a difficult period, on the information then available nobody could predict the decline that was to follow in the second half of the year.

Scotlife Homeloans (No 2) Ltd v Kenneth James & Co. (1995)

By contrast, a residential mortgage valuer was held negligent for failing either to realize or to take account of the fact that the residential property market 'had come off the boil and was falling'.

Izzard v Field Palmer (2000)

In carrying out a mortgage valuation of a maisonette in a four-storey block, a valuer failed to point out that the block was constructed under a system which combined large concrete panels and timber cladding. This omission was held to have been negligent, since the risks (of both structural problems and high maintenance charges) inherent in such construction had been thoroughly documented in the professional literature by the time the defendant carried out his inspection.

Weedon v Hindwood, Clarke & Esplin (1975)

The defendant surveyors were retained to represent the claimant property owner in compulsory purchase negotiations. Shortly before the negotiations began, a decision of the Court of Appeal altered the law as to the date on which property should be valued for compulsory purchase and, before the negotiations ended, this new ruling was confirmed by the House of Lords. The change in the law would have favoured the claimant, but the defendants agreed a figure which was clearly based on the old law. They were held to have been negligent in failing to keep their relevant legal knowledge up to date.

2.1.6 Proof of negligence

Where a court has to decide an issue of professional negligence, evidence from expert witnesses is highly persuasive. The usual practice is for each of the opposing parties to call one or more experts to give evidence on its behalf. There is also the possibility (though it is not very often used) for a court to direct that expert evidence shall be given by a single joint expert. In either case, an expert witness must possess expertise which is relevant to the matters under dispute.

Civil Procedure Rules, r. 35.7

Where two or more parties wish to submit expert evidence on a particular issue, the court may direct that the evidence on that issue is given by one expert only. Where the instructing parties cannot agree who should be the expert, the court may select the expert from a list prepared or identified by the instructing parties, or direct that the expert be selected in some other manner.

Whalley v Roberts & Roberts (1990)

In deciding whether a mortgage valuation had been negligently carried out, the court regarded evidence from a civil engineer and an architect as irrelevant. Only a surveyor could speak with authority on what could reasonably be expected from an ordinarily competent surveyor.

Sansom v Metcalfe Hambleton & Co. (1998)

In considering a building surveyor's failure to draw his client's attention to a crack in a wall, the Court of Appeal held that the trial judge had been wrong to accept the evidence of a structural engineer (who said that this amounted to negligence) in preference to that of a chartered surveyor (who said that it did not).

Abbey National Mortgages plc v Key Surveyors Nationwide Ltd (1996)

In a case involving allegedly negligent mortgage valuations of 51 properties in different parts of the country, the trial judge ordered that a single joint expert should be appointed, in addition to one expert witness appointed by each party. This was challenged by the claimants, on the ground that a single expert could not possibly have detailed knowledge of the residential market in every area concerned. However, the Court of Appeal upheld the trial judge's direction, in the belief that such a person would none the less have sufficient relevant expertise.

Where any professional person acts as an expert witness (whether or not this includes an actual appearance before a court or tribunal, or merely the preparation of a report for the purposes of litigation) that person's overriding duty is to the court, rather than to the client. The duty requires the expert to give impartial and objective evidence of his or her professional opinion.

The Ikarian Reefer (1993)

The court described the following duties of an expert witness:

- Expert evidence presented to the court should be, and should be seen to be, the independent product of the expert, uninfluenced as to form or content by the exigencies of litigation;
- an expert witness should provide independent assistance to the court by way of objective unbiased opinion in relation to matters within his or her expertise;
- an expert witness in the High Court should never assume the role of an advocate;
- an expert witness should state the facts or assumptions upon which his or her opinion is based; he or she should not omit to consider material facts which could detract from his or her concluded opinion; and
- an expert witness should make it clear when a particular question or issue falls outside his or her expertise.

Civil Procedure Rules, r. 35.3

- It is the duty of an expert to help the court on the matters within his or her expertise; and
- this duty overrides any obligation to the person from whom he or she has received instructions or by whom he or she is paid.

RICS Practice Statement: *Surveyors Acting as Expert Witnesses* (2000)

- The primary duty of the surveyor is to the judicial body to whom his evidence is given;
- the duty is to be truthful as to fact, honest and correct as to opinion and complete as to coverage of relevant matters; and
- the surveyor's evidence must be independent, objective and unbiased. In particular, it must not be biased towards the party who is responsible for paying him or her. The evidence should be the same whoever is paying for it.

Stanton v Callaghan (1998)

It was held by the Court of Appeal that, in view of an expert witness's overriding duty to the court or tribunal, he or she is immune from liability in negligence to the client in respect of evidence actually given or reports prepared for use in court.

2.2 VALUATIONS

2.2.1 The limits of a valuation

In the absence of further instructions or qualifications, a valuation should reflect the valuer's view of the open market value of the property at the relevant date. It is not the valuer's responsibility to predict future trends in property prices, except in so far as current values are already being affected by the view which the market takes of such trends.

Banque Bruxelles Lambert SA v Eagle Star Insurance Co. Ltd (1994)

The Court of Appeal emphasized that a valuer is concerned exclusively with current values, and that the purpose of a valuation is not to protect the client against a future decline in the property market.

Credit Agricole Personal Finance plc v Murray (1995)

It was suggested by the court that, notwithstanding the basic limits of a valuation, a prudent valuer should alert the client to adverse market trends of which he or she is aware.

Where a valuer is instructed to value for a particular purpose, such as mortgage lending, then it may be appropriate to base the valuation on something other than open market value. However, this does not mean that there must inevitably be a discount from the open market value in every such case – it will always depend upon market conditions.

UCB Corporate Services Ltd v Halifax (SW) Ltd (2000)

A valuer was instructed to value industrial premises (a unit in a new commercial centre) on the basis of a 90-day sale by a mortgagee in possession. He concluded that, given the evidence of local demand and recent transactions, the value of the property on this basis was exactly the same as its open market value. The Court of Appeal upheld the trial judge's finding that the valuer had not been negligent in coming to this conclusion.

2.2.2 Valuation methodology

The courts have traditionally shown themselves reluctant to be over-prescriptive as to the methods which valuers should use, although there has for a long time been general agreement about the basic procedures involved in a proper valuation. However, increased reliance on expert evidence in valuation cases has brought with it an increased awareness of the range of possible approaches to the task of valuing a property, and has also led to more detailed scrutiny of the methodology adopted by the defendant in a particular case.

Love v Mack (1905)

The court emphasized that there is not a single method of valuation, which must be strictly followed in order to avoid a finding of negligence. Even if the methods adopted by a defendant are not perfect, and not even the best that could have been selected, they may still be methods that a reasonably competent practitioner is entitled to utilize.

Corisand Investments Ltd v Druce & Co. (1978)

It was acknowledged that a valuer might legitimately base a valuation upon comparables alone, without any further calculation, or even upon his or her own experienced instinct and awareness of the market.

Singer & Friedlander Ltd v John D Wood & Co. (1977)

The court described valuation as a four-stage process:

- collecting relevant information about the property;
- analysing the information, so as to be able to accept facts and make assumptions;
- checking the findings by an appropriate alternative valuation method; and
- reporting to the client.

On the facts, the defendants had failed to make sufficient efforts to collect the necessary information (the judgment includes a detailed list of what would be relevant for this purpose).

Old Gate Estates Ltd v Toplis (1939)

It was accepted that, in normal circumstances, a valuer's duty of reasonable care and skill requires him or her to collect relevant information personally, rather than merely relying on what can be learned at second-hand.

Qureshi v Liassides (1994)

In valuing for mortgage purposes a retail greengrocery business, the defendant valuer was held negligent for failing to realize that the vendor had fraudulently exaggerated the turnover, by including a number of transactions that related to a separate business.

Strover v Harrington (1988)

In carrying out a building survey for the potential purchaser of a farmhouse, the defendant surveyor accepted the vendor's word that the property had main drainage (when in truth it had a septic tank). This was held not to have been negligent, since such information would normally be ascertained through a preliminary enquiry between solicitors. Moreover, to check the destination of the drainage would require a special test, something which the purchaser had been offered and had declined.

Banque Bruxelles Lambert SA v Eagle Star Insurance Co. Ltd (1994)

The court stated that, where a property to be valued has recently been sold, the sale price is potentially the best available 'comparable'. A valuer who is aware of the sale price but who fails to take it into account will normally be held negligent, unless there is clear evidence to show either that the sale in question did not take place at market value (for example, because the property was not properly marketed), or that the valuer was specifically instructed by the client to ignore it.

Interallianz Finanz AG v Independent Insurance Co. Ltd (1997)

A valuer who knows that the property has recently been sold, but is not aware of the sale price, will be negligent if he or she does not take all reasonable steps to discover that price, in order to take it into account in the valuation.

2.2.3 Valuation practice

Whether or not a valuer has been guilty of negligence is a question of fact, dependent on all the available evidence. This means that decided cases do not create precedents in the strict sense. They may nevertheless be of some interest and usefulness, in providing examples of the kind of conduct that has attracted judicial criticism in the past.

United Bank of Kuwait v Prudential Property Services Ltd (1994)

The defendants carried out a valuation of a completed development, a former public house refurbished as retail and office premises. They were held negligent in having miscalculated rental values in the area and in failing to make any allowance for the fact that part of the property was over-rented.

Nykredit Mortgage Bank plc v Edward Erdman Group Ltd (1993)

The defendants were held negligent in their residual valuation of a development site, on the basis that they had taken an unreasonably optimistic view of the likely demand for office accommodation in the area and had also miscalculated the potential costs of the proposed redevelopment.

BNP Mortgages Ltd v Goadsby & Harding Ltd (1994)

The defendants were held negligent in their valuation of a residential property for remortgage purposes, on the ground that they had failed adequately to consider recent sales (and aborted sales) of directly comparable neighbouring properties.

Birmingham Midshires Building Society v Richard Pamplin & Co. (1996)

The defendant carried out a mortgage valuation of a maisonette, which was situated in an area with which he was not very familiar. He was held negligent in failing to make up for his lack of local knowledge by carrying out extensive local enquiries, since these would have revealed suitable comparables.

Merivale Moore plc v Strutt & Parker (1999)

The defendants, in valuing a development property which was held on a lease with 46 years to run, adopted a yield of 7.5%. The Court of Appeal held that the defendants were not negligent in selecting this figure; however, they were negligent in failing to warn their developer clients that, in view of the absence of suitable comparables (that is, properties on medium-term leases) the choice of an appropriate yield was a more than usually risky exercise.

Zubaida v Hargreaves (1995)

The defendant, who was appointed to act as an independent expert in carrying out a rent review on restaurant premises, was held not to have been negligent, despite the claimant's argument that he had paid an unreasonable degree of attention to non-restaurant comparable properties.

Lewisham Investment Partnership Ltd v Morgan (1997)

The defendant, who was appointed to act as an independent expert in carrying out a rent review on a unit in a shopping centre, was held not to have been negligent, despite the landlords' argument that he had adopted an incorrect method of valuation. The judge in fact took the view that the earlier case law, which the defendant had followed, was wrong, but nevertheless held that a reasonable valuer was perfectly entitled to follow it.

2.2.4 The 'margin of error' or 'bracket' approach

(a) *Valuation as opinion*

The courts have, for many years, recognized that every valuation contains an element of subjective opinion, and have concluded from this that a valuer is not to be found guilty of negligence on the ground that his valuation is 'wrong' (at least where this means merely that other valuers do not agree with it).

Baxter v FW Gapp & Co. Ltd (1938)

The trial judge stated that:

> Valuation is very much a matter of opinion. We are all liable to make mistakes, and a valuer is certainly not to

be found guilty of negligence merely because his valuation turns out to be wrong.

Singer & Friedlander Ltd v John D Wood & Co. (1977)

The judge said that:

> The valuation of land by trained, competent and careful professional men is a task which rarely, if ever, admits of precise conclusion ... Valuation is an art, not a science. Pinpoint accuracy is not, therefore, to be expected.

Banque Bruxelles Lambert SA v Eagle Star Insurance Co. Ltd (1994)

It was acknowledged by the Court of Appeal that: 'Different competent valuers will produce different opinions.'

Zubaida v Hargreaves (1995)

It was said by the Court of Appeal that:

> In an action for negligence against an expert, it is not enough to show that another expert would have given a different answer. Valuation is not an exact science; it involves questions of judgement on which experts may differ without forfeiting their claim to professional competence.

(b) *Inaccuracy as negligence*

While error in itself does not amount to negligence, there comes a point at which a substantial error may raise serious doubts as to whether the valuation has been carried out with reasonable care and skill. Indeed, it now appears that such an error goes further, raising a presumption of negligence which the valuer must rebut if he or she is not to be held liable.

Baxter v FW Gapp & Co. Ltd (1938)

The Court of Appeal stated that 'gross overvaluation, unless explained, may be strong evidence either of negligence or of incompetence'.

Singer & Friedlander Ltd v John D Wood & Co. (1977)

For the first time, a court (relying upon evidence put forward by expert witnesses) explicitly recognized the idea of a 'margin of error' or 'bracket' around the true value of the subject property. The judge stated:

> There is, as I have said, the permissible margin of error, the 'bracket' as I have called it. What can properly be expected from a competent valuer using reasonable skill and care is that his valuation falls within this bracket.

The effect was that 'any valuation falling outside ... the bracket brings into question the competence of the valuer and the sort of care he gave to the task of valuation'.

Lewisham Investment Partnership Ltd v Morgan (1997)

In an action against a valuer who had acted as an independent expert on a rent review, the judge stated explicitly that, even if none of the specific allegations of negligence were established, the claim could still succeed if it were shown that the valuer's overall figure was outside the permissible bracket.

Legal & General Mortgage Services Ltd v HPC Professional Services Ltd (1997)

The judge said that, as soon as a valuation is shown to fall outside the bracket, the claimant will have discharged an evidential burden. It is then for the defendant to prove that, even though his valuation is outside the range within which careful and competent valuers may reasonably differ, he none the less exercised the appropriate degree of skill and care.

Merivale Moore plc v Strutt & Parker (1999)

The Court of Appeal, having quoted with approval the statement in the case noted above, stated that, where a valuation is shown to be outside the acceptable limit, that may be a 'strong indication' that negligence has in fact occurred. However, the court also made it clear that this does not provide *conclusive* proof of negligence.

Arab Bank plc v John D Wood (Commercial) Ltd (2000)

In the opinion of the Court of Appeal, the mere fact that a valuation is outside the margin is not conclusive evidence of negligence. But 'the evidential onus to disprove an inference of negligence shifts emphatically to the defendants, when the margin is exceeded to the extent now shown'.

(c) *Accuracy as a defence*

Although the legal position is not entirely clear, there is at least some authority for the view that, where a valuation falls within the permitted margin of error, the valuer cannot be found guilty of negligence for the way in which he or she arrived at that figure.

McIntyre v Herring Son & Daw (1988)

The judge refused to accept that there is any proposition of law that in valuation cases a valuer is not negligent if his valuation falls within the bracket.

Mount Banking Corporation Ltd v Brian Cooper & Co. (1992)

The judge stated:

> If the valuation that has been reached cannot be impeached as a total, then, however erroneous the method or its application by which the valuation has been reached, no loss has been sustained because … it was a proper valuation.

Lewisham Investment Partnership Ltd v Morgan (1997)

The judge stated explicitly that, even if one or more specific allegations of negligence against a valuer were proved, the valuer would still escape liability if the valuation fell within the permitted bracket.

Merivale Moore plc v Strutt & Parker (1999)

The Court of Appeal expressed the view that a valuer could not be liable for negligence unless his or her valuation fell outside the acceptable bracket.

Arab Bank plc v John D Wood (Commercial) Ltd (2000)

A Court of Appeal consisting of different judges expressed the view that, even where a valuation fell within the permitted bracket, a valuer might be held liable for negligence in respect of some discrete error (such as a failure to make a specific deduction for the presence of asbestos) which fed through 'pound for pound' into the final figure.

(d) *The appropriate 'bracket'*

In deciding upon the appropriate 'margin of error' in any particular case, the court will rely heavily upon the evidence of expert witnesses. The bracket which is selected depends upon the court's perception of the difficulty of the valuation task, involving such factors as the type of property, the availability of suitable comparables and the difficulty of market conditions at the time. In most cases, the figure falls between +/– 10% and +/– 15% of the 'true value', although there are examples of both wider and narrower brackets being adopted.

Singer & Friedlander Ltd v John D Wood & Co. (1977)

The court accepted that, in general, the permissible margin of error would be 10% either side of the 'right figure', but that this could be extended in exceptional circumstances to 'about 15%, or a little more, either way'.

Corisand Investments Ltd v Druce & Co. (1978)

The parties agreed that 15% was an appropriate margin of error on a valuation of a hotel.

Mount Banking Corporation Ltd v Brian Cooper & Co. (1992)

The parties agreed that 17.5% was an appropriate margin of error on a residual valuation of office premises intended for redevelopment.

Private Bank & Trust Co. Ltd v S (UK) Ltd (1993)

On a particularly difficult residual valuation, carried out against the background of a sharply falling market, the defendants' valuation was expressed as a range of between £1.35m and £1.45m. The parties agreed that the valuer was entitled to a further margin of error of 15% around this bracket.

Nykredit Mortgage Bank plc v Edward Erdman Group Ltd (1993)

A valuer's expert witness suggested a bracket of 18.7% on a particularly difficult residual valuation. However, the judge refused to allow more than 15%.

Nyckeln Finance Co. Ltd v Stumpbrook Continuation Ltd (1994)

On another, equally difficult, residual valuation, the parties' expert witnesses agreed that a bracket of only 10% was appropriate.

Arab Bank plc v John D Wood (Commercial) Ltd (2000)

On a 'franking valuation' of a large and complex industrial estate, the parties' expert witnesses agreed that it would be appropriate to allow a margin of error of 20%. They also agreed that, had the valuers been instructed to carry out a full valuation, a smaller margin of error would have been appropriate.

BNP Mortgages Ltd v Barton Cook & Sams (1996)

The parties' expert witnesses agreed that, on a valuation of a standard house on an estate, a bracket as small as 5% might be appropriate.

Axa Equity & Law Home Loans Ltd v Goldsack & Freeman (1994)

The judge applied a bracket of about 5.1% to the valuation of a leasehold flat, even though he acknowledged that there were very few true comparables available.

Credit Agricole Personal Finance plc v Murray (1995)

The judge adopted a bracket of 15% on a difficult mortgage valuation of a residential property (a substantially renovated Grade II listed building).

Scotlife Homeloans (No 2) Ltd v Kenneth James & Co. (1995)

Again, the judge adopted a bracket of 15% on a difficult mortgage valuation of a residential property, which had been converted from a row of stables.

Legal & General Mortgage Services Ltd v HPC Professional Services Ltd (1997)

On a difficult mortgage valuation of a house with an unusually large plot, the judge adopted a bracket equating to approximately 14.3%.

The Mortgage Corporation v Halifax (SW) Ltd (1999)

On a valuation of a very expensive house in Bishop's Avenue, Hampstead, the judge adopted a bracket equating to approximately 15.5%.

2.3 SURVEYS

Negligence, in the context of a survey or other inspection, almost invariably consists of the surveyor's failure to draw attention to some physical defect in the property. As to the reason for that failure, most claims are based on an allegation that the surveyor has failed to exhibit the standard of care and skill to be expected from a reasonably competent member of the profession in one or more of the following respects:

- the surveyor did not inspect the relevant part of the property at all;
- the surveyor did not carry out a proper inspection of the relevant part of the property;
- the surveyor did not understand the significance of what his or her inspection revealed; or
- the surveyor did not adequately report on what was discovered.

2.3.1 Type and extent of inspection

A surveyor may be instructed to carry out a range of inspections which differ widely in extent and depth, from a mortgage valuation to a full building survey. In order to decide whether the surveyor has shown reasonable skill and care, it is first necessary to identify the particular type of inspection involved. This may require interpretation of the surveyor's instructions, which will be an easier task if those instructions are in writing.

RICS *Appraisal and Valuation Manual*, Practice Statement 2

Members of the RICS are required by their professional body to ensure that their instructions are either in writing or confirmed in writing.

Cross v David Martin & Mortimer (1989)

The court accepted that, while a House Buyers Report and Valuation may be more limited in scope than a full building survey, a surveyor who is instructed to carry out such an inspection will be expected to show the same level of expertise as is required for a full survey.

Fisher v Knowles (1982)

The judge found that what the defendant had been instructed to carry out was something more than a bare mortgage valuation but less than a structural survey. He was to provide a report on the general state of the property and to draw attention to those matters which might give rise to suspicion, as, for example, springing floors or a musty smell, requiring further investigation in the nature of a structural survey.

Kerridge v James Abbott & Partners (1992)

The court held that, even where there is no express term of engagement limiting what will be inspected, a surveyor is under no duty to remove stonework from a parapet wall in order to inspect a concealed part of a roof.

Bishop v Watson, Watson and Scoles (1972)

The court held that a surveyor who has agreed to make a visual survey

> is under no obligation to uncover those parts of the building where the flashings or damp-proof courses should be found to see if they are there and, if they are, whether they are adequate ... evidence that the building is of cavity construction is not itself ground for suspecting that the safeguards essential to that mode of construction have been omitted or botched.

Howard v Horne & Sons (1990)

The court held that, where a surveyor reported that 'electrical wiring is in PVC cable', this implied that it was modern and gave no cause for concern. Since, in reality, much of the wiring was old, exposed and dangerous, the surveyor was held liable in negligence, despite an express clause stating that services would only be visually inspected where accessible and that they would not be tested.

Heatley v William H Brown Ltd (1992)

A surveyor who could not gain access to the roof voids of a house pointed this out in his report, which described the property as 'in reasonable condition for its age'. He was held negligent in not advising his client to delay the purchase until an inspection of the roof voids could be carried out.

The most limited type of inspection to have received judicial attention is that comprised in a mortgage valuation.

Bere v Slades (1989)

The court described the duty of a surveyor carrying out a mortgage valuation as 'not to miss obvious defects or defects which are observable by careful visual examination'. The defendant was therefore not negligent in failing to discover that certain walls were of non-standard and unstable construction, since this could not have been detected by a visual surface examination of the property.

Roberts v J Hampson & Co. (1989)

The judge accepted that a mortgage valuation involves a limited inspection, normally taking no more than half an hour, which would not allow for moving furniture or lifting carpets. However, the judge cautioned that the root of the surveyor's obligation is the taking of reasonable care and that, if a proper inspection of a particular property required two hours, this is something the surveyor must accept.

Lloyd v Butler (1990)

The judge, who agreed that a mortgage valuation should on average take no more than 20–30 minutes, described it as 'effectively a walking inspection by someone with a knowledgeable eye, experienced in practice, who knows where to look ... to detect either trouble or the potential form of trouble'.

Nash v Evens & Matta (1988)

It was held that, given the limited nature of a mortgage valuation, a surveyor who did not discover wall-tie failure had not been negligent.

Gibbs v Arnold Son & Hockley (1989)

The court accepted that, on a mortgage valuation, a surveyor's duty in respect of the roofspace is limited to carrying out a 'head and shoulders' inspection.

Ezekiel v McDade (1994)

The court accepted that, in carrying out a mortgage valuation, a surveyor should make a 'head and shoulders' inspection of the roofspace. Whether or not the defendant in this case did so was not clear (though the judge thought it unlikely), but he was in any event held negligent for not having reported on defects which would have been visible on such an inspection.

2.3.2 Surveying methods

Where it is the way in which a surveyor carried out an inspection which is called into question, the court will be heavily influenced by the evidence of expert witnesses and any relevant guidance from professional bodies.

Fryer v Bunney (1982)

The defendant, in carrying out a building survey, was held negligent for not having made sufficient use of a damp meter.

Eley v King & Chasemore (1989)

The defendants, in carrying out a building survey, inspected the inside of the roof and found no sign of water penetration. The Court of Appeal held that they had not been negligent in limiting their external inspection of the roof to what could be seen from the ground, rather than obtaining and using a long ladder to reach the roof itself.

Hacker v Thomas Deal & Co. (1991)

A building surveyor who did not use a torch and mirror to check for damp behind kitchen cupboards was held not to have been negligent, since the relevant RICS guidance specifically treated the use of a mirror as a matter of individual choice.

Pfeiffer v E & E Installations (1991)

By contrast, where a specialist firm was instructed to test a central heating system which was at the end of its normal life expectancy, the firm was held negligent for not using a torch and mirror to check for possible cracks in the heat exchanger.

Whalley v Roberts & Roberts (1990)

The judge accepted expert evidence to the effect that, on a mortgage valuation, a surveyor would not normally be expected to carry and use a spirit level.

Cormack v Washbourne (1996)

The defendant, in carrying out a building survey of a house for potential purchasers, reported that cracks which he had discovered were sufficiently serious to merit further investigation. The Court of Appeal held that, despite reporting in such terms, the surveyor had been negligent in not examining the geological survey map of the area. Had he done so, he would have warned the purchasers that the house might well be built on clay, in which case they would have withdrawn from the purchase.

Watts v Morrow (1991)

The court was highly critical of a building surveyor who dictated his full report while on site, rather than (in accordance with the relevant RICS guidance), dictating notes and producing a formal report from these at a later stage. In the judge's view, this resulted in a report which was lengthy and diffuse, strong on immediate detail but negligently lacking in reflective thought.

2.3.3 The trail of suspicion

Even where the type of inspection being carried out is one which does not, in principle, require any uncovering or opening up of concealed parts of the property, it does not automatically follow that a surveyor cannot be held negligent for failing to discover hidden defects. The crucial question is whether what was visible in the property was sufficient to alert a reasonably competent surveyor to the possibility of those defects. If so, then he or she may be under a duty to take further steps.

Roberts v J Hampson & Co. (1989)

The judge acknowledged that, in carrying out a mortgage valuation, a surveyor is not normally expected to move furniture or to lift carpets. However, he stated that, if there is some specific ground for suspicion and the trail of suspicion leads behind furniture or under carpets, the surveyor must take reasonable steps to follow the trail until he has all the necessary information. The defendant here was held negligent on this basis for failing to follow up clear signs of damp and thus to discover a serious problem.

Sneesby v Goldings (1995)

A surveyor carrying out a mortgage valuation of a converted house noticed that a chimney breast in the kitchen had been removed, and checked the room above for signs of distress (of which there were none). The Court of Appeal held that the surveyor had been negligent; had he looked inside the cooker hood or kitchen cupboards (something which he would not normally be expected to do on a limited inspection of this kind) he would have realized immediately that the chimney had been left inadequately supported.

Hipkins v Jack Cotton Partnership (1989)

The court adopted the 'follow the trail' approach in the context of a building survey. It was held that cracks in the rendering of a house, together with the slope of the nearby land, should have raised serious questions in the mind of a reasonably prudent surveyor as to the ground on which the property was built.

Hingorani v Blower (1976)

The judge accepted that, where a property has been subject to very extensive redecoration and modernization, this may itself give a surveyor reason to check carefully that the vendor has not sought to conceal serious defects (in this case, subsidence sufficiently severe to require underpinning).

Lloyd v Butler (1990)

In a case involving a mortgage valuation, the judge said that 'follow the trail' is not to be taken literally. A surveyor does not necessarily have to follow up every trail to discover whether there is trouble or the risk of trouble. But where there is evidence of actual or potential trouble, the surveyor must report in a way which clearly alerts the client, and anyone else who is entitled to rely on the report, to the risk.

Eley v King & Chasemore (1989)

A building survey report drew attention to a tall fir tree close to the house and the attendant risk of subsidence, and advised the purchaser to obtain insurance against ground movement. The Court of Appeal held that the surveyor had not been negligent in failing either to investigate further or to advise his client against purchasing. On the contrary, the surveyor had fulfilled his duty to the purchaser by giving him perfectly sound advice.

2.3.4 Particular problem areas

Allegations of negligence in the course of a survey can relate to any type of defect in the property. However, certain categories of defect have tended to give rise to more claims than others, and are more likely than others to result in liability for the surveyor.

(a) *Timber defects*

Lloyd v Butler (1990)

A mortgage valuer was held liable in negligence for failing to discover serious woodworm infestation. There was considerable doubt as to whether the valuer ought reasonably to have detected the infestation in the floorboards, since these were at least partly covered. However, the evidence suggested that an inspection of the cupboard under the stairs would have shown sufficient signs of infestation to justify calling in specialists.

Hacker v Thomas Deal & Co. (1991)

In holding that a surveyor had not been negligent in failing to detect dry rot, since the signs of this would not have been apparent at the time of his inspection, the judge pointed out that dry rot has a distinctive smell 'with which one would expect a surveyor, even of limited experience, to be familiar'.

Watts v Morrow (1991)

A surveyor reported that the first floor of an old farmhouse was generally sound and satisfactory, while noting that fitted carpets and furnishings had made a detailed inspection impossible. This was held negligent, since there was evidence (loose and defective floorboards and a sloping floor) which should have pointed to the need for further inspection.

> If the defendant had said that because of the limited nature of the inspection he could not express any view about the floor, he could not have been criticized ... On the inspection he did make, he could not reasonably express the views which he did express.

(b) *Damage due to ground movement*

Daisley v BS Hall & Co. (1972)

A surveyor was held negligent in that he should have real-ized that a row of trees near the house were poplars, and should then have gone on to discover that the house was built on shrinkable clay.

Morgan v Perry (1973)

The defendant surveyor was held negligent in not detecting serious subsidence and settlement. The court held that he should have been alerted by the steeply sloping site, clear evidence of subsidence in the adjoining road and the fact that the house, which was only four years old, had been exten-sively repointed.

Cross v David Martin & Mortimer (1989)

It was held that a surveyor carrying out a House Buyers Report and Valuation should have considered the possibility of floor slab subsidence, in view of the fact that the house was built on clay and on a slope, and that there were poplar trees nearby. Had he considered the possibility and thus inspected more carefully, he would have discovered the pres-ence of a large hump in the hall, noticeable to both the eye and the tread, which would have provided further evidence of the subsidence.

Henley v Cloke & Sons (1991)

A mortgage valuer observed noticeable distortion of bay windows, but concluded that this was of long standing and probably due to bomb blast damage during the Second World War. He was held negligent for not having discovered further symptoms of what was in fact serious subsidence, namely distorted brickwork, cracks in the return wall, distor-tion of the roof over the bay, and a displaced gully and a leaking drain.

(c) *Construction defects*

Allen v Ellis & Co. (1990)

A surveyor was held negligent for describing the detached garage of a house as 'brick built in 9-inch brickwork and in satisfactory condition', when it was in fact built of breeze block and had a 50-year-old corrugated asbestos roof which was brittle, fragile and in need of replacement.

Marder v Sautelle & Hicks (1988)

A surveyor was held negligent for failing to detect and report that the outer walls of a bungalow were built of blocks of cement and aggregate, the aggregate consisting of mine waste or 'mundic', a substance which was known to be liable to deteriorate and eventually crumble.

Peach v Iain G Chalmers & Co. (1992)

A mortgage valuer was held negligent for describing a house as 'concrete block built, harled', when it was in fact a 'Dorran' type, constructed of thin precast reinforced concrete panels bolted together.

Hooberman v Salter Rex (1985)

A surveyor was held negligent for failing to detect and warn of serious defects in the roof terrace of a maisonette, including inadequate felt upstands and the absence of zinc or lead wall flashings. The roof void beneath the terrace was also unventilated which, together with water penetration, led to a serious attack of dry rot.

Gardner v Marsh & Parsons (1997)

A surveyor was held negligent for failing to discover that the conversion of a five-storey terrace house into maisonettes and flats had been defectively carried out, with the result that floor joists had been overloaded and consequently sagged. It was held that a reasonably competent surveyor would have been sufficiently alerted by the rucking of wallpaper in one of the rooms to have investigated further, whereupon he would have discovered other less obvious signs confirming the problem.

Smith v Eric S Bush (1990)

A mortgage valuer noticed that chimney breasts in two first-floor rooms had been removed, but did not check (by a simple 'head and shoulders' inspection of the roof space) whether the chimneys had been given adequate alternative support. They had not, and one collapsed through the main bedroom some 18 months later. The valuer was held negligent.

Sneesby v Goldings (1995)

A mortgage valuer noticed that there was a chimney breast in the living room but none in the kitchen below. He accordingly looked for signs of structural movement around the remaining chimney breast and found no evidence of any such movement. However, the valuer was held negligent for not also checking in the room below to see whether a chimney breast had been removed. Had he done so, he would have found that this was in fact the case and that the chimney had been left without adequate support.

3
Extent of Liability

3.1 GENERAL PRINCIPLES

3.1.1 The purpose of an award of damages

When a court awards damages for negligence against a negligent surveyor or valuer, the basic approach which is adopted is that of seeking to put the claimant, as far as money can do it, in the position that he or she would have been in if there had been no negligence.

Beaumont v Humberts (1990)

Where a surveyor's negligent advice on reinstatement cost leads a client to under-insure property, the surveyor will be liable for the difference between what the client receives on an insurance claim and what would have been received if the property had been insured at the correct value.

Whitley (FG) & Sons Ltd v Thomas Bickerton (1993)

A surveyor, who had been representing a client in an attempt to secure planning permission for mineral extraction, negligently failed to appeal in time against a refusal of planning permission. The surveyor was held liable for the difference in value, at the moment when it became too late to appeal, between what the site was actually worth and what it would have been worth if an appeal had been lodged.

Rajdev v Becketts (1989)

A surveyor, in representing a tenant at a rent review, negligently failed to make proper representations to the independent expert, with the result that the rent was fixed at a very high level. It was held that the tenant's damages should be based on the difference in capital value between a lease at the rent fixed by the independent expert and a lease at the rent which ought to have been fixed if proper representations had been made.

3.1.2 Causation and remoteness

In order for a claimant to be awarded damages, the court must be satisfied that the defendant's breach of duty caused or contributed to the claimant's loss. In the context of a negligent survey or valuation, this means that the loss must be shown to have resulted from reliance on the advice given. Moreover, the principle of remoteness of damage means that a claimant cannot recover damages for any item of loss which could not reasonably have been foreseen as a consequence of negligence.

Thomas Miller & Co. v Richard Saunders & Partners (1989)

Surveyors acting for a tenant at a rent review negligently failed to draw certain relevant evidence to the attention of the arbitrator. It was nevertheless held that they were not liable to their client, since the court was satisfied that, even if the evidence in question had been presented to the arbitrator, he would have reached exactly the same decision as to the rent.

Allen v Ellis & Co. (1990)

A surveyor who inspected a house on behalf of a prospective purchaser negligently stated that the garage was in a satisfactory condition, when he should have reported that the corrugated asbestos roof of the garage was in a dilapidated and brittle state. A year after moving in, the purchaser stood on the roof to investigate a leak, fell through it and was injured. It was held, somewhat surprisingly, that what the purchaser had done was a foreseeable consequence of the surveyor's negligence, so that the surveyor was liable for his injuries.

3.1.3 **Reliance**

A particular aspect of the requirement of causation is that, where a surveyor or valuer is sued over an allegedly negligent report, the claimant must be shown to have relied on that report. If there is no such reliance, then the report cannot be said to have caused the claimant's loss. 'Reliance' in this context is a question of fact, and there are many borderline decisions.

Banque Bruxelles Lambert SA v Eagle Star Insurance Co. Ltd (1994)

A claim by a commercial mortgage lender against a negligent valuer failed, because the court was convinced that the lender had not really believed the valuation, but had nevertheless gone ahead with the loan for purely commercial reasons. However, a second claim, relating to a loan on another property, was not defeated by showing that the lender's agreement to lend was conditional upon obtaining mortgage indemnity guarantee insurance; this did not mean that the lender was not also relying on the valuation.

Charterhouse Bank Ltd v Rose (1995)

Where a lending bank asked valuer A to check and confirm an earlier valuation provided by valuer B (which valuer A duly did), it was held that the bank had relied on *both* valuations in reaching their decision to lend on the property.

Housing Loan Corporation plc v William H Brown Ltd (1997)

Where a lender's practice is to obtain two independent valuations of the property, and then to lend on the basis of the lower one, the lender may nevertheless be said to 'rely' on the higher one as well in reaching a lending decision. This is because, without the higher valuation, no loan would have been made.

Cavendish Funding Ltd v Henry Spencer & Sons Ltd (1998)

A lender, having obtained two independent valuations, inexplicably based its lending decision on the higher of the two. It was held that, while the lender's conduct might be described as unreasonable, it had nevertheless sufficiently relied on the valuation for the valuer to be held liable for the consequences.

Clonard Developments Ltd v Humberts (1999)

By contrast, where a property company purchased a development property on the basis of the higher of two independent valuations, it was held that the company had not truly relied on the higher valuation.

Kenney v Hall, Pain & Foster (1976)

A vendor who had come to believe (with good reason) that the defendant estate agents had substantially over-valued his property, was nevertheless held to have 'relied' sufficiently on the valuation to render the defendants liable. This was on the basis that the vendor had made allowances for his doubts, and had left what he thought would be an adequate safety margin in the asking price.

Western Trust & Savings Ltd v Strutt & Parker (1998)

The defendants valued for lending purposes certain property which was in the course of redevelopment. When the loan agreement was ultimately drawn up, the property on which it was secured included most but not all of what had been valued. In spite of this, it was held by the Court of Appeal that the lender had sufficiently 'relied' on the valuation in agreeing to lend.

Shankie-Williams v Heavey (1986)

Where the vendor of a flat commissioned a report from a dry rot specialist for the purpose of showing it to prospective purchasers, it was held that the negligent specialist was not liable to the purchaser, since there was no evidence to show that the latter had either seen the report or learned of its contents before agreeing to purchase the property.

3.1.4 Interest

Supreme Court Act 1981, s. 35A (1)

Where a court gives judgment for damages, it has a discretion to award simple interest on all or any part of the damages for all or any part of the period between the date when the claimant's cause of action arose and the date of judgment. (As to when a cause of action arises for this purpose, see section 4.2 below.)

3.2 LIABILITY TO PURCHASERS

3.2.1 The basic measure of damages

It is sometimes argued that, where a purchaser would not have agreed to buy a property had it not been for a negligent survey, the purchaser should be entitled to recover damages based on the cost of repairing all the defects which the surveyor ought reasonably to have discovered. However, the law does not take this view, basing damages instead on the difference between what the property is actually worth in its defective condition and what the purchaser has been led by the negligent survey to pay for it.

Philips v Ward (1956)

A house was purchased for £25,000, following a negligent survey which failed to reveal timber infestations. The cost of repairing these defects at the date of purchase would have been £7,000, but the true value (even with the defects) at that date was £21,000. The Court of Appeal held that the purchaser was entitled to damages of £4,000, not £7,000 – the higher figure would in effect have allowed the purchaser to acquire a house worth £21,000 for £18,000.

Perry v Sidney Phillips & Son (1982)

The Court of Appeal confirmed that the correct measure of damages in cases involving a negligent survey is the difference between the price paid and the true value. The court further ruled that this difference is to be assessed as at the date of purchase, not the date of judgment.

Watts v Morrow (1991)

A house was purchased for £177,500, following a negligent survey which failed to reveal a number of defects. The cost of repairing these defects at the date of purchase would have been £34,000, but the true value (even with the defects) at that date was £162,500. The Court of Appeal held that the purchaser was entitled to damages of £15,000, not £34,000 – the higher figure could only have been justified if the surveyor had *guaranteed*, as a term of the survey contract, that the property was free of any defect not mentioned in his report.

Patel v Hooper & Jackson (1999)

The Court of Appeal confirmed that the measure of damages described above ('difference in value' rather than 'cost of repair') is also the correct one to adopt in cases involving a negligent mortgage valuation.

While the basic principle now seems well established by the cases noted above, its precise application to the facts of a particular case may still give rise to uncertainties.

Steward v Rapley & Co. (1989)

The Court of Appeal expressed its agreement with the measure of damages described above. However, the court accepted that, when it comes to establishing the 'true value' of a defective property, it may be quite legitimate to begin with its value in an apparently undamaged condition and then to deduct the cost of necessary repairs from that figure. If this approach to valuation is adopted, it will effectively result in the same figure for 'difference in value' as would have been produced by 'cost of repair'.

Hardy v Wamsley-Lewis (1967)

A house was purchased for £4,600, following a negligent survey which valued it at £4,300. Its true value at the date of purchase (due to defects which the survey should have revealed) was only £3,500. It was held that the purchaser's damages should be £800 rather than £1,100, since the purchaser could hardly be said to have relied on the valuation in deciding to pay an extra £300.

Oswald v Countrywide Surveyors Ltd (1996)

A house was purchased for £225,000, following a negligent survey which valued it 'in the region of £215,000'. Its true value at the date of purchase (due to defects which the survey should have revealed) was only £165,000. The Court of Appeal accepted the finding of the trial judge that the purchasers' decision to pay £225,000 was attributable to the surveyors' negligence, even though it exceeded their valuation of the property. Damages were accordingly assessed at £60,000, rather than £50,000.

Shaw v Halifax (SW) Ltd (1996)

The defendants, in carrying out a mortgage valuation at a time when the housing market was rising sharply, placed a value of £37,000 on a house which was at that time worth only £32,000. Two months later, the claimant purchased the house for £42,000, by which time its actual value had risen to £37,000. The defendants argued that the claimant had suffered no loss, but the Court of Appeal upheld an award of £5,000 damages.

The courts' insistence on applying the 'difference in value' principle can occasionally lead to some surprising results.

Hooberman v Salter Rex (1985)

A surveyor negligently failed to discover dry rot and, as a result, the house was purchased for more than its true value. By the time the purchaser discovered the dry rot, the cost of the work which would be needed to rectify the problem had increased by four times. It was nevertheless held that the purchaser's damages should be based on 'difference in value' at the date of purchase.

Upstone v GDW Carnegie & Co. (1978)

The claimant purchased a house following a negligent survey by the defendants which failed to reveal certain defects. At the trial, the valuation evidence established that, notwithstanding these defects, the house had been worth what the purchaser had paid for it. The purchaser was accordingly held entitled only to nominal damages.

Daisley v BS Hall & Co. (1972)

The claimant purchased a house for £1,750 more than its true value, following a negligent survey which failed to reveal damage caused by subsoil movement. By the date of trial it was clear that the necessary remedial works would cost only £250, but the purchaser was nevertheless held entitled to £1,750 damages.

Gardner v Marsh & Parsons (1997)

The claimants acquired a long lease of a maisonette for £114,000, following a negligent survey which failed to reveal serious structural defects caused by inadequate conversion works. Its true value at the date of purchase was only £85,000. The Court of Appeal, applying the 'difference in value' principle, held that the purchasers were entitled to damages of £29,000. This was in spite of the fact, by the date of trial, the purchasers had, by threatening legal proceedings, pressurized their landlord (who had carried out the conversion) into rectifying the defects at his own expense.

3.2.2 Incidental losses and expenses

In addition to the basic measure of damages described above, a purchaser who has been misled by a negligent valuation or survey is entitled to recover compensation for other incidental losses and expenses. Precisely what these include will depend on whether the negligence is discovered in time to avoid going through with the purchase, or whether a purchaser, having completed the purchase before discovering the defects, decides to resell or to remain in the property and put right the defects which the surveyor has failed to discover.

(a) *Where no purchase results*

Buckland v Watts (1968)

A purchaser, after he had exchanged contracts but before completion, discovered that a survey had negligently failed to reveal defects in the property. He thereupon refused to complete the purchase. The purchaser was held entitled to recover damages from the surveyor in respect of the deposit which he forfeited to the vendor and also his wasted conveyancing costs.

(b) *Where purchaser resells*

Patel v Hooper & Jackson (1999)

A purchaser who had relied on a negligent mortgage valuation discovered, on moving in, that the house was so defective as to be virtually uninhabitable. He was held entitled to recover the cost of alternative accommodation for himself and his family until such time as he could sell the house and acquire another property.

Watts v Morrow (1991)

It was accepted by the Court of Appeal that a purchaser who, on discovering a surveyor's negligence, chooses to resell the property is entitled to recover damages in respect of the legal and other costs incurred in moving into and out of the property.

Ezekiel v McDade (1994)

It was held that damages for legal and other costs incurred in moving into and out of a defective property are similarly recoverable by a purchaser who is forced to leave because the house is repossessed by a mortgage lender.

(c) *Where purchaser repairs*

It is clear from the cases outlined above that a purchaser is not entitled to recover compensation for the cost of repairing defects which the surveyor or valuer ought reasonably to have discovered. Nevertheless, it seems to be generally accepted by the courts that compensation may be recovered for certain expenses which are incidental to the repairing process, provided that these are not properly to be regarded as part of the cost of repair itself.

Morgan v Perry (1973)

A purchaser recovered damages in respect of costs incurred in investigating defects which the surveyor had negligently failed to discover.

Broadoak Properties Ltd v Young & White (1989)

A company which purchased defective property as a result of a negligent survey was awarded damages to cover the cost of management time wasted in investigating defects.

Treml v Ernest W Gibson & Partners (1984)

A house purchaser recovered damages for the cost of temporary works which were carried out on an emergency basis to render the property safe.

Cross v David Martin & Mortimer (1989)

A house purchaser who chose to remain in and repair a defective property was held entitled to the cost of alternative accommodation and furniture storage during the period when repairs were carried out.

Hill v Debenham Tewson and Chinnocks (1958)

A surveyor, who negligently failed to warn house purchasers to postpone redecoration work until a damp problem had been rectified, was held liable for the purchasers' wasted expenditure on plastering and decoration.

3.2.3 Compensation for inconvenience

A surveyor or valuer whose negligence causes physical (not merely mental) inconvenience or discomfort to the claimant may be liable to pay damages as compensation for this. Since the essence of the claim is physical inconvenience (most commonly the result of having to live for a substantial time in defective and uncomfortable conditions), it appears that commercial occupiers cannot recover such damages. The amount of damages awarded under this head are usually modest.

Watts v Morrow (1991)

A contract-breaker is not in general liable for any distress, frustration or displeasure which the breach of contract causes to the innocent party, except where the very object of the contract is to provide pleasure, relaxation or peace of mind. The Court of Appeal held in this case that a contract to survey a house for a prospective purchaser does not normally fall within this exception, with the result that a negligent surveyor is liable only for *physical* inconvenience and discomfort resulting from the surveyor's breach of contract.

Farley v Skinner (2001)

A surveyor was instructed to inspect a house for a prospective purchaser and was specifically asked to investigate whether the property was affected by aircraft noise. He negligently failed to do so, and the purchaser found that his enjoyment of the property was indeed affected by such noise (although the noise was not sufficient to affect the value of the property). The House of Lords held that this was an exceptional case, where an important object of the contract was to provide pleasure, so that the surveyor was liable to pay damages (assessed at £10,000) for the fact that the purchaser suffered exactly the kind of displeasure he had tried to avoid. Alternatively, the House of Lords held that the noise was a sufficiently physical interference to be treated as 'inconvenience and discomfort'.

Goodwin v Phillips (1994)

In what appears to be the highest award to date of damages under this head, a diabetic husband and wheelchair-bound wife received £12,500 for the extreme physical inconvenience suffered over a period of more than two years in a seriously defective house, followed by a further four years in unsuitable alternative accommodation, namely a mobile home.

3.3 LIABILITY TO VENDORS

Where a valuer negligently undervalues property on behalf of a prospective vendor, with the result that the property is sold for less than its market value, the basic measure of damages consists of the difference between the true value of the property and the price at which it has been sold in reliance on the valuer's advice. However, while this is the most common type of loss resulting from a negligent valuation for a vendor, it is not the only one, and other measures of compensation may sometimes be appropriate.

Weedon v Hindwood, Clarke & Esplin (1975)

The defendant valuers, in conducting compulsory purchase negotiations with a local authority, negligently advised their client to accept a price for his property which was too low. The valuers were held liable to the client for the difference between the price which he agreed to accept and the price which ought to have been achieved.

Kenney v Hall, Pain & Foster (1976)

The claimant, relying on a valuation of his house from the defendants, put it on the market at what appeared to be a reasonable price and acquired two other properties by means of a bridging loan. The house, which had been negligently over-valued by the defendants, proved virtually impossible to resell, and the very substantial interest charges incurred by the claimant almost led to his bankruptcy. The evidence established that, had the claimant been properly advised, he would have embarked on a much more modest scheme which, due to a fall in the property market, would have resulted in a loss of £10,000. Damages were therefore assessed to cover all the claimant's losses, save for the £10,000 which would have been lost in any event.

3.4 LIABILITY TO LENDERS

Where a mortgage lender has lent and lost money in reliance on a negligent valuation, a court which is asked to assess damages for the lender must first answer, on the basis of the available evidence, the following question: if the valuer had not been negligent (and had therefore furnished the lender with an accurate valuation of the property), would a mortgage loan, albeit a smaller one, still have been made? If the answer to this question is yes, then the case is a 'smaller transaction' or 'successful transaction' one. If, however, knowledge of the property's true value would have resulted in no mortgage taking place, then this is a 'no transaction' case. The reason for making this distinction is that, in a 'smaller transaction' case, the lender's damages must not include any losses which would have been suffered in any event on the hypothetical smaller loan (that is, because the market has fallen). This is because such losses cannot be said to have been caused by the valuer's negligence; they would still have occurred if he or she had not been negligent.

3.4.1 Damages in 'smaller transaction' cases

Corisand Investments Ltd v Druce & Co. (1978)

Where, given an accurate valuation, a smaller mortgage loan would have been made, the basic measure of damages consists of whatever the lender has actually lent and lost, minus anything the lender would still have lent and lost on the hypothetical smaller transaction. The lender will not normally be entitled to recover the costs of repossessing and reselling the mortgage property, since it is assumed that these costs would equally have been incurred on the smaller transaction.

The Mortgage Corporation v Halifax (SW) Ltd (1999)

Where, in a 'smaller transaction' case, the borrower has repaid part of the loan before defaulting, this must be taken into account in calculating the lender's total loss on the mortgage loan. However, the court should also make a finding as to what repayments would have been made on the hypothetical smaller loan, in order to assess what sum is to be deducted from the total loss in order to arrive at the correct measure of damages.

3.4.2 Damages in 'no transaction' cases

Where a lender can show that, had it not been for a negligent over-valuation of the subject property, there would have been no loan at all, the lender is in principle entitled to recover compensation for all the losses which it has incurred as a result of entering into the mortgage transaction. Notwithstanding the contrary view which has been expressed in a number of cases, this can include losses which have come about because of a fall in market values generally between the date of mortgage and the date on which the mortgaged property is repossessed and resold. However, this is subject to a very important qualification: the total damages awarded against the negligent valuer cannot exceed the amount of the over-valuation, that is the difference between the negligent valuation provided by the defendant and the true value of the property at the date of that valuation.

(a) *The 'cap' on liability*

South Australia Asset Management Corp. v York Montague Ltd (1996)

The House of Lords held that a person (such as a valuer) who is under a duty to take reasonable care to provide information on which someone else (such as a lender) will decide upon a course of action, is, if negligent, not responsible for all the consequences of that course of action being taken. He or she is responsible only for the consequences of being wrong. Thus, where a valuer had over-valued property by £10m, the lender was entitled to recover its total loss of £9.25m on the loan transaction. However, where a valuer had over-valued property by £1.5m, the lender was entitled only to recover this amount, rather than the £3m which the lender had actually lost.

Nykredit Mortgage Bank plc v Edward Erdman Group Ltd (No 2) (1998)

The House of Lords explained the reasoning behind the 'cap' on a valuer's liability as follows:

> The valuer is not liable for consequences which would have arisen even if his advice had been correct. This is because they are the consequences of risks the lender would have taken upon himself if the valuation advice had been sound. As such they are not within the scope of the duty owed to the lender by the valuer.

As stated above, provided only that the 'cap' is not exceeded, a lender is entitled to recover damages for the total loss suffered. In assessing this 'total loss', a number of elements must be taken into account. These include the capital sum lent, interest on that capital and any incidental costs incurred in repossessing and reselling the security. Against this must then be set the value of the property when realized, any money recovered from the borrower and the value of any other rights acquired by the lender as part of the mortgage transaction.

(b) *Damages for loss of interest*

Swingcastle Ltd v Alastair Gibson (1991)

A finance company, relying on a negligent over-valuation of a house, lent to high-risk borrowers at a rate of interest of 36%, rising to 45% immediately on any default in repayment.

When the borrowers defaulted, the lender repossessed and resold the property and then sued the negligent valuer for its total losses, including interest at the stipulated contractual rate. The House of Lords rejected this part of the lender's claim (on the basis that it would effectively put the valuer in the position of a guarantor of the borrowers' repayment obligations), ruling that the lender was entitled instead to damages reflecting the reasonable costs which it had incurred in financing the loan.

HIT Finance Ltd v Lewis & Tucker Ltd (1993)

In the absence of evidence as to precisely how a group of finance companies had raised the money for its mortgage lending activities, it was held that the damages payable by a negligent valuer should include interest at a normal commercial rate.

The Mortgage Corporation v Halifax (SW) Ltd (1999)

It was held that, since it would be reasonably foreseeable that a lending institution might be financing its mortgage lending by borrowing money at compound interest, the damages payable by a negligent valuer should include interest assessed on a compound basis.

(c) *Incidental losses and expenses*

In principle, damages in a 'no transaction' case should include all costs properly and reasonably incurred by the lender in repossessing and reselling the mortgaged property on the borrower's default.

Swingcastle Ltd v Alastair Gibson (1991)

A lender was held entitled to recover what it had paid to estate agents and solicitors for their services in respect of repossession proceedings and subsequent resale.

HIT Finance Ltd v Lewis & Tucker Ltd (1993)

A lender was held not entitled to recover in respect of money which it had paid to the estate agents who handled the resale of mortgaged property. This was because, on examination of the estate agency agreement, it was found that this had been a 'sympathy payment', not one which the lender had been under a legal obligation to make.

(d) *Offsets against damages*

Having calculated the total amount (including interest) paid out by the lender, the court must then deduct from this any money or other property which the lender has actually received. This will of course include whatever is recovered on resale of the mortgage property; if the property has still not been resold by the date of trial, then the lender must instead give credit for its value at that date.

London & South of England Building Society v Stone (1983)

The Court of Appeal held that, in assessing the total loss suffered by the lender, credit must be given for any repayments made by the borrower before default.

Banque Bruxelles Lambert SA v Eagle Star Insurance Co. Ltd (1994)

It was held that, where property which has been repossessed by the lender produces income (such as rent) before it is resold, this too must be taken into account in calculating the lender's total loss.

It is clear that, in addition to what has actually been received, the lender must also give credit for the value of any rights which it has acquired as part of the mortgage transaction. The most important of these is likely to be the lender's right to enforce the borrower's obligations to repay the mortgage loan. However, while the courts agree that this right is to be taken into account, there has been no clear agreement as to how this should be done.

Eagle Star Insurance Co. Ltd v Gale and Power (1955)

A lender claimed damages in respect of a negligent over-valuation at a time when the borrower had not defaulted in his repayments and there were no indications that he was likely to do so. Moreover, the terms of the mortgage stipulated for repayment of approximately one-half of the capital (£1,500 out of a loan of £3,015) after four years and, if this duly took place, the value of the property would provide ample security for the remaining loan. The judge accordingly awarded the lenders £100 damages as compensation for what was perceived to be a fairly small risk, namely that the borrower might yet default in making the agreed repayment.

London & South of England Building Society v Stone (1983)

A valuer, in inspecting a house for mortgage purposes, negligently failed to discover that it was in imminent danger of collapsing due to subsidence and was thus effectively worthless. The lender, having repossessed the property, decided to take no action against the borrowers under the mortgage (a loan of £11,800) and sued the valuer for its total loss. The trial judge held that the lender ought reasonably to have mitigated its loss by pursuing the borrowers for at least part of the debt, and accordingly reduced the damages by £3,000. However, a majority of the Court of Appeal ruled that the lender's decision had been a reasonable one in the circumstances and that there should accordingly be no reduction in the damages awarded.

Nykredit Mortgage Bank plc v Edward Erdman Group Ltd (No 2) (1998)

The House of Lords held that the correct approach in such cases is not to apply the principle that the lender has a duty to take reasonable steps to mitigate its loss, but rather to recognize that the 'borrower's covenant to repay the mortgage loan' has a capital value which is to be offset against the total loss suffered by the lender.

DNB Mortgages v Bullock and Lees (2000)

The court ruled that the value of a borrower's covenant to repay is simply a question of fact. Here, at a time when the borrower had not yet defaulted, it was held that his covenant to repay should be valued at less than £10,000.

Lloyds Bank v Burd Pearce (2000)

In this case the court adopted a more technical approach to the valuation of the borrower's covenant to repay, by comparing the borrower's total assets with his total liabilities at the relevant time.

(e) *Interest on damages*

Quite apart from the part played by interest in assessing the lender's total loss (see section b above), a lender, like any other successful claimant, may be entitled to simple interest on the damages awarded, for all or any part of the period from the date when the cause of action arose to the date of judgment. This is by virtue of the Supreme Court Act 1981, s. 35A (see section 3.1.4, above).

Nykredit Mortgage Bank plc v Edward Erdman Group Ltd (No 2) (1998)

The House of Lords held that, in a 'no transaction' case, interest of this kind should run from the date on which the lender's loss reaches the level of the 'cap' (that is, when the total loss, assessed in accordance with the principles described above, is equivalent to the amount by which the property has been negligently over-valued). Until that position is reached, the lender is entitled to interest as part of the damages; that is to say, interest at a reasonable commercial rate, which will go towards making the total loss reach the 'cap'.

4
Defences

4.1 DISCLAIMERS AND EXEMPTION CLAUSES

4.1.1 General principles

As a matter of principle, a surveyor or valuer is perfectly entitled to exclude or restrict his or her potential liability to the client for negligence, by means of an appropriate term in the contract between them. Such a term might seek to exclude liability altogether, or to restrict it in some way (for example, by the imposition of a financial ceiling or a time limit within which a claim must be brought). In order to be effective, such a term must satisfy both the common law rules which govern exemption clauses in contracts and also the provisions of the Unfair Contract Terms Act 1977. In particular, the common law requires the term in question to have been incorporated into the contract from the beginning and to have been brought sufficiently to the notice of the client. The statute creates an additional requirement of reasonableness.

Although it is not technically an exemption clause, an apparently similar method of protecting a surveyor or valuer is by means of some qualification in the report to the client, intended to limit the latter's reliance on that report (for example, by emphasizing the limits of the inspection that has been undertaken). In order to be effective, such a qualification must be clearly expressed.

Lowy v Woodroffe, Buchanan and Coulter (1950)

The defendant surveyors stated in their report on a house that 'in view of the prevalence of dry rot in London it is impossible to guarantee every property is free'. It was held that this did not protect the surveyors from a claim that they had negligently failed to discover dry rot in the property.

Surveyors and valuers frequently attempt to avoid any liability to third parties, by inserting a clause in their reports stating that they undertake no responsibility to anyone other than the person to whom the report is addressed. Once again, such clauses are subject to both common law and statutory rules.

Commercial Financial Services Ltd v McBeth & Co. (1988)

The defendant valuers provided a property developer with a report on a proposed development. The report stated: 'This valuation is for the use only of the parties to whom it is addressed and no responsibility is accepted to any third party'. It was held that the valuers owed no duty of care to a mortgage lender who was shown the report and who relied on it in reaching the decision to lend.

Omega Trust Co. Ltd v Wright Son & Pepper (1997)

The defendant valuers provided a property owner with a valuation which contained a clause stating: 'This report shall be for private and confidential use of the clients.' However, the valuers subsequently agreed that the report could be readdressed to a named lender. The Court of Appeal held that the valuers owed a duty of care to this lender, but that the disclaimer was effective to rule out a claim by a second financial institution, which became a joint lender by providing part of the mortgage funds.

Hadden v City of Glasgow DC (1986)

On applying to a local authority for a mortgage loan, a house purchaser was shown a clearly worded disclaimer of liability in respect of the mortgage valuation. It was held that this prevented the implication of any duty of care owed by the mortgage valuer to the purchaser.

Martin v Bell-Ingram (1986)

A house purchaser who applied to a building society for a mortgage loan was shown a clearly worded disclaimer in respect of the mortgage valuation. However, this was not done until after the applicant had relied on the mortgage valuation and had exchanged contracts to purchase. It was held that the disclaimer came too late to prevent the implication of a duty of care owed by the mortgage valuer to the purchaser.

4.1.2 The Unfair Contract Terms Act 1977

Under this Act, attempts to exclude or restrict certain types of contractual and tortious liability are completely ineffective, while attempts to exclude or restrict other types of liability are subject to a statutory test of reasonableness.

Unfair Contract Terms Act 1977, s. 2 (1)

A person cannot by reference to any contract term or notice exclude or restrict his liability for death or personal injury resulting from negligence.

Unfair Contract Terms Act 1977, s. 2 (2)

In the case of other loss or damage (that is, damage to property or financial loss) a person cannot so exclude or restrict his liability for negligence except in so far as the term or notice satisfies the requirement of reasonableness.

Unfair Contract Terms Act 1977, s. 11 (1)

In relation to a contract term, the requirement of reasonableness is that the term shall have been a fair and reasonable one to be included having regard to the circumstances which were, or ought reasonably to have been, known to the parties when the contract was made.

Unfair Contract Terms Act 1977, s. 11 (3)

In relation to a notice, the requirement of reasonableness is that it should be fair and reasonable to allow reliance on it, having regard to all the circumstances obtaining when the liability would have arisen.

Smith v Eric S Bush (1990)

A house purchaser who applied to a building society for a mortgage loan signed a form which clearly disclaimed any assumption of responsibility on the part of the mortgage valuer. The House of Lords held that this disclaimer was subject to the test of 'reasonableness' imposed by the Unfair Contract Terms Act and, moreover, that it failed that test. This was because the house purchaser was, at least indirectly, paying for the mortgage valuation (and should not have to pay to duplicate that information by commissioning his own inspection), and because the task of the valuer was 'at the lower end of a surveyor's field of expertise'. However, the House of Lords made it clear that a different decision might be justified in cases involving large commercial properties (and possibly also very expensive residential properties). Here it might well be reasonable for a mortgage valuer to exclude or restrict liability to someone who was, after all, not a client.

Stevenson v Nationwide Building Society (1984)

This earlier case concerned the purchase by an estate agent of a property which comprised two shops, a maisonette and a flat. It was held that a disclaimer of responsibility by the mortgage valuer was fair and reasonable, apparently because the property was not simply a modest residential one and because the purchaser was someone who would be familiar with this type of disclaimer and with the range of surveys and valuations available.

Omega Trust Co. Ltd v Wright Son & Pepper (1997)

As noted above, valuers who had provided a lender with a valuation marked 'for private and confidential use of clients' sought to rely on this clause to avoid liability to a second lender, to whom the report was shown and who relied on it in deciding to enter the transaction as a joint lender. The Court of Appeal held that the clause was a fair and reasonable one. This was on the grounds that the parties were of equal bargaining power; that the second lender could easily have commissioned its own valuation; and that a professional valuer, valuing expensive properties in a commercial context, was entitled to know who his client was and to whom his duty was owed.

4.2 TIME LIMITS

For every type of legal action, the Limitation Act 1980 lays down a time limit within which the claimant must start proceedings. Failure to do so will mean that the claim is statute-barred and is thus doomed to fail. As far as professional negligence is concerned, some claims (by clients) are based on breach of contract and others (by clients or third parties) are based on tort. In any given case, the cause of action (that is to say, contract or tort) will determine both the length of the limitation period and the date from which it begins to run.

4.2.1 Claims in contract

Limitation Act 1980, s. 5

An action founded on simple contract shall not be brought after the expiration of six years from the 'date on which the cause of action accrued'. This has been interpreted by the courts to mean the date on which the defendant is guilty of a breach of contract.

4.2.2 Claims in tort

The limitation rules governing negligence actions based on tort are complicated. The Limitation Act lays down an 'overriding time limit', after which proceedings are finally barred (except in cases of 'deliberate concealment' as described below). Until that period expires, a claimant is entitled to bring proceedings provided that he or she is still within one or other of two shorter periods laid down by the Act. These two periods are alternatives, in the sense that a claimant is entitled to start proceedings while either of them is still running, even though the other one may have expired.

(a) *The overriding time limit*

Limitation Act 1980, s. 14B

An action for damages for negligence, other than one involving a claim for personal injuries, shall not be brought after the expiration of fifteen years from the last date on which there occurred an act or omission which is alleged to constitute negligence (that is, the last breach by the defendant of his or her duty of care).

(b) *The basic period*

Limitation Act 1980, s. 2

An action founded on tort shall not be brought after the expiration of six years from the 'date on which the cause of action accrued'. This has been interpreted by the courts to mean the date on which the claimant suffers loss or damage as a result of the defendant's negligence. In cases involving a survey or valuation, the relevant date will vary according to what it is that the claimant has done in reliance on the allegedly negligent report.

Byrne v Hall Pain & Foster (1999)

The purchasers of a flat brought an action for negligence in respect of a mortgage valuation, commissioned by the lenders, on which they had relied. Proceedings were commenced more than six years after the claimants had exchanged contracts to purchase, but less than six years after the purchase was completed. The Court of Appeal held that the date on which the purchasers suffered loss, and thus triggered the start of the basic limitation period, was the date on which they exchanged contracts to purchase, since it was then that the purchasers were legally committed to pay more for the flat than it was truly worth. Their claim was therefore statute-barred.

Secretary of State for the Environment v Essex, Goodman & Suggitt (1985)

The claimants, having taken a lease of a large office block, brought an action for negligence against the surveyors who had inspected the property for them. It was held that the basic limitation period began on the date when the claimants were irrevocably committed to taking the lease.

Nykredit Mortgage Bank plc v Edward Erdman Group Ltd (No 2) (1998)

The House of Lords held that, where a mortgage lender sues a valuer for negligence, the lender's loss (and therefore the start of the basic limitation period) occurs at the first moment that the lender is not fully secured. This is when the amount outstanding on the mortgage (that is, the capital debt plus whatever interest has accrued) exceeds the value of the lender's rights (that is, the value of the security plus the value of the borrower's undertaking to repay the loan). In a case where the property has been seriously over-valued, this may occur as soon as the mortgage loan is made. Where this is not so, it will be necessary to track both the amount outstanding and the value of the lender's rights, until the point is reached at which the lender is no longer fully secured.

Gulf Oil (Great Britain) Ltd v Phillis (1998)

A tenant brought an action against the surveyor who had been appointed to act as an independent expert under a rent review clause, alleging that he had negligently determined too high a rent. It was held that the tenant's loss, and therefore the start of the basic limitation period, occurred when the tenant first paid rent at the new level.

Whitley (FG) & Sons Ltd v Thomas Bickerton (1993)

The claimants, who had conditional planning permission for gravel extraction, brought an action against the surveyors who acted as their advisers, alleging that they had negligently allowed the planning permission to lapse. It was held that the claimants' loss, and therefore the start of the limitation period, occurred at the first moment when the deteriorating planning prospects for the site had become sufficiently obvious to have an adverse effect on its value.

(c) *Latent damage*

Limitation Act 1980, s. 14A

This section lays down an alternative limitation period for claims in negligence, in cases where a claimant's cause of action accrues before he or she is aware of it. In effect, the claimant is entitled to start legal proceedings within three years of the date on which he or she has knowledge of the 'material facts' about the damage which has been suffered. These are defined as

> such facts about the damage as would lead a reasonable person to consider it sufficiently serious to justify instituting proceedings against a defendant who did not dispute liability and was able to satisfy a judgment.

It is further provided that the claimant is deemed to have knowledge which he or she might reasonably be expected to acquire from facts observable or ascertainable by him or her, with the help of appropriate expert advice where it would be reasonable to seek this.

Spencer-Ward v Humberts (1995)

The Court of Appeal stated that 'knowledge', for this purpose, does not mean 'know for certain and beyond possibility of contradiction'. It means know with sufficient confidence to embark on the preliminaries to legal proceedings such as submitting a claim to the defendant, seeking legal and other advice and collecting evidence. Vague and unsupported suspicion is not enough, but reasonable belief will be.

Finance for Mortgages Ltd v Farley & Co. (1996)

Where lenders became aware that the police were investigating suspected mortgage fraud in relation to a property on which they had lent money, it was held that a reasonable lender would have repossessed the property and would then have discovered negligence by the mortgage valuer. The three-year period therefore ran from the date on which this should have been done.

Campbell v Meacocks (1995)

House purchasers brought an action against the mortgage valuer who had inspected the property on behalf of the lender, alleging that he had negligently failed to discover subsidence. It was held that the mere fact that the claimants knew that an adjoining house had suffered from subsidence was not enough to fix them with knowledge of 'material facts' about their own damage and thus to start the three-year period.

Horbury v Craig Hall & Rutley (1991)

The claimant purchased a house in reliance on a survey commissioned from the defendants. After moving in, the claimant realized that the defendants had negligently failed to discover that certain chimney breasts had been removed, leaving the flues without proper support. It was held that this defect, which was put right by the claimant at a cost of £132, was serious enough to justify a reasonable person in instituting proceedings, and that it therefore operated to trigger the three-year period. It was further held that, once the period had expired, it operated so as to bar any claim arising out of the negligent survey (not just a claim in respect of the missing chimney breasts). Thus, when the claimant later discovered that the surveyor had also overlooked serious dry rot, a claim in respect of this was statute-barred.

Hamlin v Edwin Evans (1996)

The claimants, before purchasing a house, commissioned a House Buyers Report and Valuation from the defendants. A year after moving into the property, the claimants discovered dry rot which the defendants had failed to detect, and brought a claim against the defendants which was settled. Five years later, the claimants discovered that the defendants had also failed to detect serious damage due to subsidence and they started legal proceedings in respect of this damage. However, the Court of Appeal held that the claimants' discovery of the first defect operated to trigger the three-year period in respect of all claims, with the result that the later one was statute-barred.

4.2.3 Deliberate concealment

Limitation Act 1980, s. 32

Where any fact relevant to a claimant's right of action has been deliberately concealed by the defendant, the normal limitation period does not begin to run until the claimant has discovered the concealment or could with reasonable diligence have discovered it. For this purpose, 'deliberate concealment' includes deliberate commission of a breach of duty in circumstances where it is unlikely to be discovered for some time.

Brocklesby v Armitage & Guest (2001)

The Court of Appeal held that there can be 'deliberate concealment' where a person does a deliberate act which amounts to a breach of duty, whether or not the person is aware of the legal consequences of the act.

Sheldon v RHM Outhwaite (Underwriting Agencies) Ltd (1996)

The House of Lords held that s. 32 does not require the defendant's breach of duty to be concealed from the time that it is committed. It can also apply where concealment occurs at a later date, even when the original limitation period is about to expire and (possibly) even after it has expired. The effect of such concealment is to start a new six-year period running from the date of discovery.

Westlake v Bracknell DC (1987)

The claimants purchased a house with the aid of a mortgage from the defendant local authority, after a mortgage valuation had been carried out by one of the defendants' employed surveyors. Shortly after moving in, the claimants discovered signs of structural movement and notified the local authority, whereupon the same surveyor reinspected the property and assured the claimants that all structural movement had ceased. When the claimants later brought an action for negligence in respect of the original inspection, it was held that the conduct of the surveyor on his return visit amounted to 'deliberate concealment'.

5
Shifting the Blame

5.1 MITIGATION OF DAMAGE

Under the principle of mitigation, a person who seeks damages for breach of contract or in tort is precluded from recovering compensation for any aspect of the loss or damage which he or she could have avoided by taking reasonable steps. Such loss or damage is regarded in law as having resulted entirely from the claimant's own failure to mitigate, rather than from the defendant's breach. The onus of proving that the claimant has failed to take reasonable steps to mitigate his or her loss lies on the defendant. In the context of negligence claims against surveyors or valuers, the issue of mitigation can arise in a variety of ways.

5.1.1 Claims by purchasers

Patel v Hooper & Jackson (1999)

The claimants, relying on a negligent House Buyers Report and Valuation from the defendants, purchased a house which was found to be virtually uninhabitable. The claimants were awarded damages on the basis of 'difference in value' (see section 3.2.1, above) plus compensation for the cost of alternative accommodation up to the time that they ought reasonably to have resold the defective property. The Court of Appeal pointed out that the claimants' duty to mitigate required such a resale, not just in order to avoid the risk of a further depreciation in its value but also to put a limit on the period during which the defendants would be liable to compensate them for the costs of their alternative accommodation.

Cross v David Martin & Mortimer (1989)

The claimants purchased a house in reliance on a House Buyers Report and Valuation from the defendants, who had negligently failed to discover movement of the concrete slab caused by subsidence. When this defect subsequently came to light, the necessary investigative work meant that the claimants lived for four years with a large hole in their hall. However, their claim for general damages for the inconvenience (on which see section 3.2.3 above) was rejected by the judge, on the ground that they should have mitigated this loss by effecting temporary repairs to the hole.

5.1.2 Claims by lenders

Nyckeln Finance Co. Ltd v Stumpbrook Continuation Ltd (1994)

The claimants, relying on a valuation from the defendants, lent £21m to fund the purchase of a large office block. The borrowers defaulted in repayment at a time when the market was falling rapidly, but the claimants delayed for almost a year in taking steps to repossess the property, despite the fact that in August 1990 they received an offer of £17m for it. When the property was finally repossessed and resold, it realized only £3.1m. It was held that, in assessing damages, the claimants were not entitled to be compensated for any loss that would have avoided if they had sold the property for £17m in August 1990.

London & South of England Building Society v Stone (1983)

As noted in section 3.4.2 d above, it was held by a majority of the Court of Appeal that a lender's decision not to take legal action against a house owner, who failed in mortgage repayments, did not constitute an unreasonable failure by the lender to mitigate its loss. The lender was accordingly entitled to recover damages in full from a negligent mortgage valuer.

Nykredit Mortgage Bank plc v Edward Erdman Group Ltd (No 2) (1998)

As also noted in section 3.4.2 d above, the House of Lords cast considerable doubt on the idea that a lender's failure to take legal action against the defaulting borrower can be a matter of mitigation. It was held that the correct approach in such cases is instead to recognize that the 'borrower's covenant to repay the mortgage loan' has a capital value, and that this value is to be offset against the total loss suffered by the lender.

5.2 CONTRIBUTORY NEGLIGENCE

A valuer or surveyor who is sued for negligence may, and frequently does, raise the defence that the claimant's loss has resulted, at least in part, from the claimant's own fault. If the court is satisfied that this is indeed so, it does not mean that the claimant's case fails altogether. Instead, the damages awarded will be reduced to take account of the relative contributions of the parties.

Law Reform (Contributory Negligence) Act 1945, s. 1

Where any person suffers damage as the result partly of his own fault and partly of the fault of any other person or persons, the damages recoverable shall be reduced to such an extent as the court thinks just and equitable having regard to the claimant's share in the responsibility for the damage.

Law Reform (Contributory Negligence) Act 1945, s. 4

'Fault', for the purpose of the Act, means negligence, breach of statutory duty or other act or omission which gives rise to liability in tort or which would have given rise at common law to a defence of contributory negligence.

Platform Home Loans Ltd v Oyston Shipways Ltd (1999)

The House of Lords held that, where a negligent valuer's liability to a lender is subject to a 'cap' equal to the amount by which the property has been over-valued (see section 3.4.2 a above), any reduction of the damages on the ground of the lender's contributory negligence is to be made from the lender's total loss, rather than from the 'cap'. In this case the lender had lost £611,000, damages were 'capped' at £500,000, and the lender was 20% responsible. The Court of Appeal awarded the lender damages of £400,000 (that is, £500,000 less 20%) but the House of Lords held that this was wrong and that the correct measure damages was £489,000 (that is, £611,000 less 20%).

5.2.1 Scope of the defence

The court undoubtedly has power to apportion liability on the ground of the claimant's own fault where an action is brought in the tort of negligence. The extent to which the power exists in other types of action is less clear.

Forsikringaktieselskapet Vesta v Butcher (1986)

It was held that the statutory defence of contributory negligence cannot be used in an action for breach of a strict contractual duty (that is, one where liability is independent of negligence). Nor is it available in an action for breach of a contractual duty of care between parties whose relationship is such that no concurrent duty would arise in tort. However, the defence *can* be raised in an action for breach of a contractual duty of care where there is a concurrent duty in tort. This will normally be the case in an action for professional negligence.

Alliance & Leicester Building Society v Edgestop (1994)

It was held that contributory negligence cannot be used as a defence to an action based on fraud, even by a defendant who is not personally guilty of dishonesty (for example, where an innocent employer is made vicariously liable for the fraud of an employee).

Reeves v Commissioner of Police of the Metropolis (1999)

Some doubt has been cast on the ruling in the case noted immediately above by the House of Lords' decision in this case, which concerned a suicide attempt by a person in police custody who was known to have such tendencies. The House of Lords held that the claimant (who alleged that the police had in effect negligently failed to protect him from himself) was guilty of contributory negligence. In so deciding, the court interpreted 'fault' under the 1945 Act in such a way as to include intentional as well as careless conduct.

5.2.2 The claimant's fault

The 1945 Act does not seek to define or categorize the type of conduct that may amount to contributory negligence. However, cases of professional negligence involving valuers or surveyors are almost invariably based on one of three kinds of allegation:

- that the claimant helped to cause the defendant's error;
- that the claimant acted unreasonably in relying on the defendant's report; or
- that the claimant's decision to enter into the loss-making transaction was imprudent for other, independent, reasons.

(a) *Claimant's contribution to the erroneous advice*

Craneheath Securities Ltd v York Montague Ltd (1994)

The defendants, in valuing a restaurant, were negligent in taking an unrealistic view of the turnover. The valuers had not seen any recent accounts of the business; however, it emerged that the claimants themselves had obtained a recent set of accounts, but had not shown these to the valuers. It was held on the facts that the defendants had not been negligent; however, the judge expressed the opinion that, had negligence been established, the claimants' conduct would probably have led to a finding of contributory negligence.

South Australia Asset Management Corp. v York Montague Ltd (1996)

The defendants carried out a valuation of a large development site for the claimants, who had been approached to finance the development. There was considerable confusion as to the precise service which the defendants were to carry out, in particular whether or not they were to provide an open market valuation. This confusion arose, at least in part, because the claimants, contrary to their own internal lending guidelines, did not provide direct and explicit instructions to the defendants as to what they required. It was held that this failure on the part of the claimants amounted to contributory negligence.

Western Trust & Savings Ltd v Strutt & Parker (1998)

The defendants carried out a valuation of a holiday development scheme which, through failure to discover a planning problem, resulted in a negligently high figure. The Court of Appeal held that this failure resulted, at least in part, from the way in which the claimant lenders permitted the borrower to instruct the valuers, together with the way in which they had instructed their own solicitors. Taken together, these faults of the claimants were held to justify a reduction of 25% in the damages awarded.

(b) *Claimant's unreasonable reliance on the advice*

In a number of cases, commercial mortgage lenders have been held guilty of contributory negligence for relying blindly on a valuation, in circumstances where the valuation itself gave rise to some reasonable doubt. However, the courts have proved far less willing to apply a similar principle to cases involving private individuals.

Banque Bruxelles Lambert SA v Eagle Star Insurance Co. Ltd (1994)

The claimants, in agreeing to lend on the security of various commercial properties, relied on valuations of those properties carried out by the defendants, very shortly after the properties had been acquired by the borrowers. The defendants in their reports placed values on the properties which were up to 70% above the prices at which they had been acquired, without offering any explanation for these apparently enormous rises in value. It was held that the claimants, who were equally aware of the discrepancies between the purchase prices and the valuations, were themselves negligent in failing to ask the defendants for an explanation, and were responsible for 30% of their losses.

Nyckeln Finance Co. Ltd v Stumpbrook Continuation Ltd (1994)

In this case too, the claimant lenders were aware of a substantial discrepancy between the price at which borrowers had agreed to acquire a property and the valuation placed on that property by the defendants. The claimants made at least some attempt to query this with the defendants but, when the defendants stood by their valuation, the claimants took no further steps. It was again held that the claimants were guilty of contributory negligence; here the appropriate reduction in damages was held to be 20%.

Interallianz Finanz AG v Independent Insurance Co. Ltd (1997)

The claimant lenders were aware that the property on which they were asked to lend had been very recently acquired by the borrowers, although they had no actual knowledge of the purchase price. It was held that the claimants' failure to enquire about the price, in order to compare this with the defendants' valuation, amounted to contributory negligence for which the claimants must bear 15% responsibility.

Barclays Bank plc v William H Brown Ltd (1996)

The claimant lenders were held 25% responsible for relying without question on a valuation which suggested that the subject property had increased in value by 130% in less than a year.

Cavendish Funding Ltd v Henry Spencer & Sons Ltd (1998)

As noted in section 3.1.3 above, lenders who obtained two independent valuations of a property, but who then inexplicably based their lending decision on the higher of the two, were held to have relied on this sufficiently for the negligent valuer to be liable. However, the lenders were held to have been contributorily negligent and therefore responsible for 25% of their own losses.

Yianni v Edwin Evans & Sons (1982)

In this action by house purchasers against a mortgage valuer appointed by a building society lender, the valuer alleged that the claimants were guilty of contributory negligence in that they had failed to commission their own survey (as strongly recommended in the building society literature) and had taken no other steps to investigate the condition of the house. However, these allegations were dismissed by the judge, who held that the purchasers were quite entitled simply to rely on the defendants to have made a competent inspection and valuation.

Allen v Ellis & Co. (1990)

As noted in section 3.1.2 above, the defendant surveyors negligently assured their house purchaser client that the detached garage was in satisfactory condition, when its roof was in fact brittle and unsafe. The house purchaser 'relied' on this statement as indicating that it would be safe for him to stand on the roof of the garage when investigating a leak. The judge accepted that a building survey is not a safety audit, and also noted that it was clear from the evidence that the claimant had at least some idea that what he was doing was dangerous. It was nevertheless held that the claimant was not guilty of contributory negligence.

(c) *Claimant's independent imprudence*

The cases in this category have so far all concerned mortgage lenders. Valuers have claimed that, for one reason or another, the lending policy in question is not one which a reasonably prudent lender would have operated. The two most common allegations relate to the adoption of a high loan-to-value ratio and a failure to carry out adequate checks on the financial stability of the borrower. It seems that, while a combination of these two factors may well result in a finding of contributory negligence, neither of them taken alone will be sufficient in normal circumstances.

Platform Home Loans Ltd v Oyston Shipways Ltd (1996)

The practice of the claimant lenders, when approached for a 'non-status' or 'self-certification' loan (that is, one in which no check is made on the borrower's claimed financial assets) on residential property, was to obtain two independent valuations and to lend 70% of the lower of these. This practice was held to be negligent, in that it left the lenders without a sufficient safety margin. In an action against a negligent valuer, the lender was accordingly held responsible for 20% of the losses resulting from the mortgage transaction.

Coventry Building Society v William Martin & Partners (1997)

The claimant lenders were held guilty of contributory negligence in adopting a loan-to-value ratio of 75% on a 'self-certification' loan. The appropriate share of responsibility was again assessed at 20%.

HIT Finance Ltd v Lewis & Tucker Ltd (1993)

The judge in this case acknowledged that a lender would not be acting prudently in making a loan where there was some reason to doubt the integrity of the borrower. However, the judge's view was that, where there were no grounds for suspicion, the lender could not be described as imprudent in agreeing to lend 70% of an independent valuation without further enquiries. This was because the apparent 'cushion' would be reasonably assumed to provide a substantial safeguard against such eventualities as an unpredicted market fall.

Banque Bruxelles Lambert SA v Eagle Star Insurance Co. Ltd (1994)

In a commercial lending transaction, it was held that a lender which had no reason to doubt the financial assets of the borrower was not guilty of contributory negligence merely for agreeing to lend 90% of the value of the property, as reported by an independent valuer.

Credit Agricole Personal Finance plc v Murray (1995)

It was held that a lender's decision to make a loan on a self-certification basis to a borrower, whose business affairs were very unclear and whose reported income fluctuated wildly, amounted to contributory negligence. The valuer was in fact acquitted of negligence but, if he had been liable, the judge would have reduced the damages payable by 15%.

Chelsea Building Society v Goddard & Smith (1996)

The claimants agreed to lend £1.25m, at a loan-to-value ratio of 80%, to a foreign national. In reaching this decision, the claimants relied on the management accounts of a foreign company and on what was clearly an unsatisfactory report from unqualified accountants. This was held to amount to contributory negligence, and the lenders were responsible for 25% of their losses.

Halifax Mortgage Services Ltd v Robert Holmes & Co. (1997)

The claimants agreed to lend £225,000, at a loan-to-value ratio of 75%, to a director of a property company, despite being aware that the borrower's name did not appear on the electoral register. It was held that this amounted to contributory negligence, for which the lenders were 30% responsible.

Midland Bank plc v Douglas Allen (1997)

The claimant lenders agreed to extend an existing loan to a company, provided that one of the directors executed a guarantee of repayment, backed by a charge over his house. The claimants were held contributorily negligent, and therefore responsible for 30% of their losses, for permitting the loan to be extended without ensuring that the charge had been duly executed.

5.3 CONTRIBUTION FROM THIRD PARTIES

Although it does not furnish a negligent surveyor or valuer with a defence against liability to a claimant, the Civil Liability (Contribution) Act 1978 provides a mechanism by which he or she may recoup at least part of the damages from any other negligent party (for example, the claimant's solicitors).

Civil Liability (Contribution) Act 1978, ss. 1 and 2

A person liable in respect of any damage suffered by another may recover contribution from any other person who is, or who would be if sued, liable in respect of the same damage. The amount of contribution shall be such as the court finds just and equitable, having regard to their respective shares in responsibility for the damage in question.

Theodore Goddard v Fletcher King Services Ltd (1997)

Solicitors, in drafting a lease on behalf of landlords, negligently failed to ensure that the rent review clause made provision for upwards only reviews. The draft lease was shown to the landlords' managing surveyors, who failed to notice the defect. It was held that the solicitors were entitled to recover a contribution from the surveyors; however, this amounted to only 20% of the damages, as the primary responsibility for this error lay with the solicitors.

Bristol & West Building Society v Christie & Butcher (1996)

Valuers acting for a mortgage lender negligently over-valued a property; solicitors advising on the same transaction negligently failed to report matters which cast doubt on the honesty of the borrower. It was held that a contribution of 50% would be 'just and equitable'.

Chelsea Building Society v Goddard & Smith (1996)

Valuers acting for a mortgage lender negligently over-valued a property; solicitors advising on the same transaction negligently permitted the claimants' funds to be wrongly applied. It was again held that a contribution of 50% would be 'just and equitable'.

Anglia Hastings & Thanet Building Society v House & Son (1981)

Valuers acting for a mortgage lender negligently over-valued a property; solicitors advising on the same transaction negligently permitted the claimants' funds to be wrongly applied, and also failed to disclose that the solicitors themselves had been guilty of serious conflicts of interest. It was held that the valuers were entitled to recover a contribution of 70% from the solicitors.

Ball v Banner; Neill Clerk v Healey & Baker (2000)

A firm of solicitors who launched an Enterprise Zone Property Unit Trust were held liable to investors for misleading information contained in the prospectus which they had drafted. They then sought a contribution from the valuers who had provided other, also misleading, information for the prospectus, claiming that the latter would, if sued, also have been liable to the investors. However, as described in section 3.4.2 a above, the valuers' liability would have been 'capped' at the level of their over-valuation. It was held that the solicitors and valuers were equally to blame, and that the solicitors were therefore entitled to recover a contribution equivalent to one-half of the damages for which they were liable. It was further held that this meant one-half of the total damages (provided that the resulting figure was within the 'cap'), and not one-half of the lower, 'capped', amount.

Howkins & Harrison v Tyler (2000)

Valuers who were held liable to mortgage lenders for a negligent over-valuation of the property sought to recover a contribution from the borrower, whose default had triggered the lenders' loss. The Court of Appeal held that they were not entitled to do so. This was because the borrowers' liability to the lenders was not in respect of 'the same damage' as that of the valuers, so that the Civil Liability (Contribution) Act did not apply.

Index

Index

Index